Money Matters in Medicine

Jordan D. Frey

Money Matters in Medicine

Managing Personal Finances as a Physician

 Springer

Jordan D. Frey
Department of Plastic & Reconstructive Surgery
Erie County Medical Center, University of Buffalo
Buffalo, NY, USA

ISBN 978-3-031-27299-8   ISBN 978-3-031-27300-1   (eBook)
https://doi.org/10.1007/978-3-031-27300-1

This Springer imprint is published by the registered company Springer Nature Switzerland AG
The registered company address is: Gewerbestrasse 11, 6330 Cham, Switzerland

This book is dedicated to all healthcare professionals aiming to improve their well-being, and that of their patients

Preface

Ever heard of a poor physician? I hadn't until I was one.

Ever thought that becoming a doctor meant automatic financial security? I did until all that came with my degree was debt.

Ever wonder why some doctors seem to have it all while you're trying to dig yourself out of a hole? I did until I figured out how to build my way out.

If you can relate to my struggles, then this book is for you…

Until recently, I had experienced all these thoughts. I was in my 7th year of surgical training after medical school when I realized that I was experiencing symptoms of burnout. I found it more difficult to remember why I had gotten into medicine. My medical experiences were feeling more and more depersonalized. Further, despite winning external awards and publishing prolifically, I didn't feel like I was accomplishing anything.

Realizing that I was experiencing burnout was eye-opening and quite difficult to come to grips with. Many of you may share a similar experience. It took some time, but I finally began to reflect on what was at the root of my burnout. Not surprisingly, there were many items on the list. But one kept coming up at the top…and that was money.

Here I was, at the end of my training, and finally about to become an attending plastic surgeon. Everyone was congratulating me and telling me that things were finally going to be "all good." I would finally be making good money now!

However, I didn't feel like things were all good at all. I had nearly $500,000 in student loans, credit card debt, no savings, and no investments. I had a wife and two young children. Even more, I felt pressure in becoming an attending to start collecting the items that defined (in my mind) a doctor. Things like a fancy car, huge home, custom suits, and big watches. So yes, I was finally going to make more money. But I could already feel this money evaporating into more and more debt. There didn't seem to be a way out. And I felt suffocated. This was not how I wanted to feel after all my years of sacrifice and hard work.

However, with this root cause now defined, I could act. Like so many doctors, I had actively ignored my finances—saying things like, "Money doesn't matter." I knew I made tons of financial mistakes. But they were too scary and intimidating for me to look at. Now was the time to change that.

So, my wife, Selenid, and I decided to learn about personal finance and get our finances under control. Unfortunately, this was quite challenging. But not for the reason that we thought. I feared looking at how bad I had let things get. However, once I finally did look, I felt relief, not dread. Things were bad (like net worth of -$550,000 bad), but finally facing my financial situation took the power away for my fears and back into my hands. The real challenge, however, was the time and effort it took to gather and separate all the helpful information from the unhelpful and potentially dangerous.

With time and determination, we succeeded in doing this. We created our own written financial plan, started managing all aspects of our own finances, and developed a debt pay off plan to be student debt free in 5 years. It was at this point that something happened which I did not totally expect...

I was still in training at this point. I did not make a cent more money. My net worth did not change at all. My debt remained the same ballooned amount. But I had a plan. And I knew that all I had to do was to follow this plan and I would, by definition, reach my financial goals and financial freedom—the idea that I could work and practice medicine because I want to, not because I have to. With this plan in place, my burnout began to alleviate. In fact, I noticed that I actually became a better doctor. And now that I am years out from this event, I can confirm that this relationship has only strengthened.

Suddenly, I realized that money does matter in medicine. In fact, it matters so much that it actually impacts our ability to care for patients. Every hospital system in the country is working to improve the well-being of physicians as we recognize burnout as an epidemic. But we are missing a huge part of the puzzle! Financial well-being is a critical component of overall well-being. And yet it is nearly universally ignored (for reasons, we will explore in this book)!

From this epiphany on, my mission and passion became helping all physicians improve their financial well-being to impact their overall well-being. The ultimate goal is for physicians to reach financial freedom. Not so they can retire. In fact, the most pushback I receive is from other doctors who think I am doing this because I want to retire. I love what I do! And I don't plan to retire anytime soon. But I do know that I work better when it is on my own terms. That also gives me flexibility to adapt if circumstances within healthcare change. I truly believe that a nation and world of financially free doctors could change and improve healthcare in ways that we cannot even currently imagine.

In fact, one of the best things about financial well-being is that there is never a "too early" or "too late." We all are on different schedules. I can promise you that whether you are early, mid, or late career in medicine, all the tools in this book are still as available to and effective for you as anyone else! Financial well-being, personal and professional satisfaction, and freedom of time are all in your grasp. And that is the aim...

The reason that I share this personal story first is because I know what you are going through. I've made every financial mistake in the book. I have yet to meet anyone—yes, anyone—coming out of medical training in a worse financial situation than myself. What this means is that if I can do it, so can you! And I'm not shouting instructions back from the finish line. I am right here running the same race that you are!

And that is the purpose of this book. My goal is to create a simple, straightforward, and all-in-one-place guide for physicians to improve their financial wellbeing. That way, you don't need to search all over the place and try to decipher good from bad advice like I did. You have it all right here at your fingertips.

Before we move on together and get into the substance of this book, there is one last thing that I want to address. You may be feeling a bit nervous, intimidated, or downright scared to start reading. You may also be intimidated by the topic or worried that you do not have enough time to learn this. And I get it. Because I felt the same way before starting my journey. But we all progress the same way. We have to crawl before we walk before, we run. And in that order. Think back to day 1 of intern year. Did you feel ready? Heck no! But you took it step by step and look at where you are now. This is the same thing.

My recommendation is to set a goal of reading 5 or 10 pages of the book each day. That is what I did when I started, and the habit continues for me today. Stay consistent by creating manageable chunks and expectations for yourself. If you miss a day because of a long day in the clinic or hospital, that's fine. Just get back to it the next day. Before long, the pages will be turning!

Thank you for joining me on this journey. Now let's get started!

Buffalo, NY, USA   Jordan D. Frey, MD

Acknowledgments

Writing a book like this is certainly not anything that I could do alone. And while, despite my best efforts, I will leave someone out of these acknowledgments, there are certain individuals and groups that I would like to especially thank for their support and guidance in this endeavor!

First, I would like to thank all of my clinical mentors and teachers through my medical school, residency, and fellowship training. Becoming a plastic and reconstructive surgeon and being able to care for patients in restoring form and function is my life's dream. I am deeply indebted to all of your selfless dedication to my clinical education. These include attendings and co-residents alike. There are too many to mention but you know who you are.

Next, my path to financial well-being is not walked alone. To all who read my blog at www.prudentplasticsurgeon.com, thank you. I am truly on this journey with you and draw immense inspiration and motivation in being able to share my story with you all. I continually learn from our entire community which has invigorated my passion for physician well-being and clinical medicine. You have also all served as unknowing readers and editors for much of the content of this book!

Also, to my financial mentors and colleagues, both physicians and nonphysicians, thank you for inspiring me, answering my questions, and helping me to spread my message. These include Jimmy Turner, Leif Dahleen, Daniel Shin, Ian Cook, Leti Alto and Kenji Asakura, Jim Dahle, Peter Kim, Vikram Raya, and many others.

I also need to acknowledge my clinical partners Thom Loree, Mark Burke, Michael Nagai, and Mark Falco for putting up with my incessant chatter about financial well-being and all of the preceding contents of this book.

To my family, my mother Lisa, father Bill, stepfather Joe, brother Jason, sister Alli, and brother-in-law Justin, and mother-in-law Enid, thank you for all of your unconditional support and love as I pursue these new avenues in my life. Same goes for all of my extended family.

Thank you to my wife, Selenid. You believed in me and in this vision since its inception. Your unwavering belief, encouragement, and love mean everything. You are equal partner and coauthor in this journey. Finally, to my three boys, Samuel, Emery, and Camilo, you are the "why" for all of this!

Contents

Chapter 1
Why Do Doctors Need to Know About Personal Finance?

In starting this journey together, I think the best place to start is with "why?" This will become a theme throughout this book as you will see. But for now, the question that we want to answer is, "Why do doctors need to know about personal finance?" Because you picked up this book, you may have some innate sense that finance plays a role in the success of physicians. But you may not have a fully formed theory as to why this is the case. Or maybe you are actually not sure that it matters at all. Without answering this question and believing in the answer, we cannot be successful in the journey. The path I will lay out may be simple. But that does not make it necessarily easy. Understanding just how important it is makes the journey and its destination worthwhile.

In answering our all-important "why" question, let's start by first examining why doctors have traditionally ignored their personal finances. The answers are multifactorial, but all converge into one central taboo within medicine. The taboo that caring about money makes you less of a physician. That somehow caring about your finances and caring for your patients are mutually exclusive. As you will see, they are not. But for the longest time, this misconception perfectly illustrated how I felt about money. And it served as my excuse to ignore my personal finances to my own detriment.

So why do so many physicians identify money as a source of stress while simultaneously labelling it as a forbidden topic? Here is a small representation of the various reasons provided either by me in the past or other physicians to me:

- "I did not get into medicine for the money."
- "My patients are what is important, not the money I make."
- "Medicine is a selfless field. Money corrupts that."
- "My finances will take care of themselves."
- "I have a *money person* that handles it for me, so I don't need to worry about it"

Unfortunately, all these rationalizations are cognitive distortions that misguide our relationship with money as physicians.

J. D. Frey, *Money Matters in Medicine*,
https://doi.org/10.1007/978-3-031-27300-1_1

Specifically, the first three comments usually arise from a misplaced sense of purpose and guilt. The overwhelming majority of doctors, including myself, did not get into medicine for the money. We got into medicine to help others. Like any calling, money comes as a consequence of following our passions. This makes us feel guilty. However, again we are misconstruing the relationship here. As a physician, we have two options. We can use the money we make intentionally to improve our financial well-being and become better doctors. Or we can mismanage it, leading to burnout, moral injury, and poor patient care.

Once we consider this perspective, financial well-being becomes a responsibility not just to ourselves, but to our patients. If our patients are important (*they are!*) then our personal finances are important by extension. Moreover, financial well-being and money cease to be corruptors of physicians. In fact, it is ironic that physicians with low financial well-being seem to be the ones most influenced by the money they feel they lack. In contrast, financially well doctors can selflessly care for patients regardless of external monetary pressures—they are working only because they *want to*, not because they *have to*! This is a very important distinction.

Now, let's move onto the last two common money cognitive distortions above. One of the most common refrains I hear from other doctors is "My finances will take care of themselves." The root of this distortion is most often fear. Personal finance can be a scary subject. It seems like a black box that is very important but that we could never understand. We know we have made money mistakes, but we don't even know what or how bad they are. So, instead of facing them, we hide from them behind the guise of our rationalization that "they will take care of themselves."

And lastly, it is our intimidation of the topic that leads us to seek someone else to take our finances from our hands. Before going further, let me digress to say that I have no problem with physicians using a financial advisor who offers good advice at a fair price. The issue becomes that most physicians lack the basic financial literacy to tell a good financial advisor from a bad one. (Not to mention that by the time you gain enough financial literacy to make this distinction, you have enough to manage your money by yourself…) What I am saying here is that even if you have a financial advisor, you can never just "not worry" or ignore your finances!

Now that we understand why physicians have traditionally shunned and ignored their financial well-being, it is time to examine why we actually *should* care about our personal finances and money. Let's start at a very basic level. Our job as physicians is to help others—remember, that is why we got into medicine! Let's examine what allows us to do that at our top capacity.

This is where Maslow's hierarchy of needs comes into play. Maslow's hierarchy illustrates in the form of a pyramid what humans *need* to function at their top level. The base is formed by physiologic needs—things like water, food, and air. The next level up is safety needs, followed by love and belonging, esteem, and self-actualization. The premise here is that we, as humans, cannot climb to the next rung of this pyramid before the needs of our current rung are met. It's hard to self-actualize without food security and so on.

We can easily extend this concept to physicians. To function as our best doctor selves at the top of the pyramid, there are more basic needs that must be met before we can advance. We can create an entire rung of this "Physician's Hierarchy of Needs" encompassing our overall well-being. Things like mental well-being, physical well-being, and—you guessed it!—financial well-being. It is hard to be fully present with patient care when you are not financially secure.

Without financial—and overall—well-being, doctors cannot perform to the top of their abilities. And this is in the best-case scenario. Unfortunately, the more common occurrence for physicians attempting to advance to the top of their pyramid before meeting their basic well-being needs is burnout such as that I experienced. Burnout costs the American healthcare system billions of dollars every year. But more importantly, it costs patients' and physicians' health alike in some quantifiable and more unquantifiable ways. This is unacceptable to any degree. Hopefully, the important and inextricable link between personal finance, medicine, and optimal patient care is now becoming clear!

Fortunately, the healthcare system has begun to recognize the burnout pandemic among physicians. Unfortunately, the healthcare system has not yet grasped the underlying causes leading to the symptoms of burnout. Efforts at combating physician burnout and improving well-being thus remain ineffective at best and comical at worst. However, within this perhaps well-intentioned effort to boost physician well-being by healthcare systems, there is a glaring omission.

Systems-led wellness efforts tend to focus on physical and mental well-being. Despite lacking effectiveness in most cases, these topics are rightfully highlighted. However, financial well-being is nearly universally ignored. All of this is then combined with a lack of financial education for physicians throughout our years of education and training.

Why is this? Well, at a systems-level most doctors are still beholden to the taboo that money is a dirty word for physicians that we discussed earlier. Aside from this, there is another misconception among administrators (often planning these wellness events) that to discuss money will lead doctors to selfishly seek greater compensation. This irrational belief is both unfounded and propagated even though physician compensation accounts for roughly only 8% of all healthcare expenditures.

Meanwhile at an education-level, physician-educators either believe that money is not important (*do you sense a trend...*) or that there is just too much other information to teach to-be doctors or doctors in training and not enough time to add anything else. While I do understand the time crunch within medical education, I refuse to believe that there is not enough time for a topic as important as this. My belief has been further reinforced by all the Grand Rounds talks and seminars on financial well-being that I have given to training programs and medical schools over the recent years.

Regardless, the overall effect here is that the pervasive and unhelpful money taboo is thus pushed further into the subconscious of the medical field and its players. This is despite the fact that we have soundly established that financial well-being is actually a key and not a detriment to physicians and the care we provide. We have therefore answered our initial question, "Why do doctors need to know about personal finance?" We also now understand why, despite the answer to our question, financial well-being is still too often overlooked.

The next logical question thus becomes, "What can we do about it?" And that is exactly the focus of the remainder of this book! Given the complete lack of any formal education to improve financial literacy for doctors, my journey started with hours of research, reading, analysis, planning, making mistakes, re-planning, and on and on. This book will distil all my research, mistakes, successes, and experiences into a simple, cohesive strategy for you to enact that I can guarantee will vastly improve your financial well-being, put you on a path to financial freedom, and make you a better physician.

To begin this construct, I'm going to start with what I believe to be the best teacher in life—mistakes. Mistakes are opportunities to learn, improve and rise above. And when it comes to money, I have had a lot of these opportunities! So, let's explore the top mistakes that doctors (*i.e., me*) make with their money.

Chapter 2
Top Mistakes that Doctors Make with Their Money

We all have a choice when we make a mistake or fail at something. We can let it define us, becoming a victim. Or we can learn from the mistake or failure, overcoming it in the process. For many years, I let my financial mistakes define me. As a result of my financial failures, I told myself stories like, "I am not good at money," "Money is not important," and "I can figure it out later." All these stories were excuses that I told myself to avoid having to face my mistakes. Because I was scared of them and intimidate of seeing them in the light of day.

Unfortunately, it took burnout for me to recognize that avoiding these money mistakes was not the answer. Doing so was making things worse and not better. I remained fearful and intimidated of looking at them. But I knew that the alternative was even worse. In fact, once I did look at my failures in the light of day, I did not feel the dread that I thought would come. Instead, I felt relief. Now that I confronted my failures, I could finally go about learning from them and ultimately overcoming them. I finally felt in power over then instead of the other way around.

The goal of this chapter is therefore to shine a light on the most common mistakes that doctors make with their money. Put another way, we are going to look at all the financial mistakes that I personally have made. Ideally, none of these will sound familiar to you. But the reality is that I see most physicians making some, if not all, of these mistakes quite commonly. The reason again goes back to a lack of formal financial education resulting in widespread lack of financial literacy among physicians.

By taking an in depth look at these mistakes, however, we can confront them and take power over them. Only once we have done this, we can finally begin taking the steps forward in creating our path to financial well-being and financial freedom.

The first and most pervasive financial mistake that we make as physicians is that we equate our high income with wealth. We think that because we make a lot of money that means we are rich and automatically have financial well-being. Unfortunately, nothing is further from the truth. Let's say you are an extremely high-income doctor and make $one million annually. Well, if you also spend $one

J. D. Frey, *Money Matters in Medicine*, https://doi.org/10.1007/978-3-031-27300-1_2

million annually, your wealth is zero. And if you spend more than $one million in annual expenses, your wealth is actually negative! So, the first lesson we learn from this mistake is that it is not *what you make* that matter, but *what you do with what you make.*

The example above may seem silly. You may be asking, "How could someone spend more than $1 million?!" We see this all the time with professional athletes. These are prime examples of high-income performers who outspend their massive salaries without anything left when their career, and income along with it, ends. Unfortunately, athletes are not the only high-income earners who fall victim to this trap. There is a significant percentage of physicians who continue to work beyond when they want simply because they need the income to cover their expenses. Because they made the mistake of thinking they were wealthy just because of their high income. The fallacy of this misconception hits hard when one wants to work less or stop working but realizes they still have huge expenses to cover. This is a huge cause of burnout in the middle to later career physician demographic.

This first mistake dovetails nicely into another all-too-common financial fallacy. And that is that physicians often tend to misjudge and overestimate the length of their careers. Starting out, we are eager to practice independently after years of training. We take on difficult cases out of ambition, but also because we are starting as the "new doc." In the early part of our career, we believe that we will want to keep this professional schedule for the rest of our career. Even as we progress on and may scale back a bit, physicians estimate that they can maintain prime performance well past our peak years.

As a result of this mistake, doctors often tell me that "they can just take care of their finances later." The truth however is that, while there it is never too late to start, the earlier that you take advantage of compound interest to build wealth, the better. The financial moves you make at the beginning of your journey will have a much greater impact than those later on. Couple this with the fact that our careers end, by our own decision or not, much earlier than we anticipate, and we have a recipe for financial disaster.

If these mistakes are hitting home, don't worry. They did for me too! The rest of this book will focus on how to overcome these mistakes based on tried and proven strategies. For instance, the answer to overcoming our first mistake is to recognize and learn that net worth is the proper measurement for wealth. Once we understand this, we can start playing the game in our favor. This is all covered in Chap. 6.

But for now, let's confront a few more of the biggest and most common money mistakes that we make as doctors. The next few that we will address have to do with spending money. If the simple formula to build wealth is to increase and invest the gap between what you make and what you spend, it does not come a surprise that unwise spending can seriously inhibit our journey to financial well-being.

Let's call this gap between what you make and what you spend "*the margin.*" Doctors are in general very high-income earners. That means we start out in a good position on the "what you make" side of this equation. However, it is the "what we spend" side of the equation that we are bad at and that hurts us the most. The result is that we do not create enough *margin*. I know many physicians making six figure salaries who have less *margin* than manual laborers making $60,000 annually. The reason again? Income has nothing to do with wealth building! It's not what you make, but what you keep (i.e., the margin) that matters.

Let's take this even a step further. *Why do doctors fail to create enough of a margin?* Rephrasing this question based on the margin equation described above, *Why are doctors so bad at controlling spending (also known as saving)?* There are two primary reasons: delayed gratification leading to unintentional spending and trying to live up to the popular image of a physician.

As doctors, our education and training are long and arduous. During this time, we are either taking out large amounts of debt or making little money compared to the hours we put in. Put more bluntly, we spend our nearly a decade of our prime years with little money and less time available. As a result, we build up a tremendous amount of delayed gratification for items and experiences that we cannot afford or simply don't have time for. This delayed gratification builds and builds and builds. Until 1 day, we become an attending physician. Our salary on average triples overnight. Suddenly, we have the money and time to satisfy all these delayed desires. And do we ever satisfy them!

The problem however is that humans in general are very bad at predicting ahead of time what purchases will bring us commensurate joy and fulfilment. This results in unintentional spending in which we buy something, receive a small hit of dopamine which then wears off, and we are left no more joyful or fulfilled by our purchase. So, we seek another purchase! The vicious cycle has begun. Mind you, unintentional spending is rampant among all individuals. But when you combine unintentional spending with individuals with intense delayed gratification and a sudden huge increase in income, the result is even more potent. And now mix in that we carry huge amounts of debt that then tend to take a back seat to these unintentional expenditures.

But maybe unintentional spending isn't really that bad? If we splurge for a few items or experiences with such a high income, what's the harm? Well, this may be true if the goods and services purchased unintentionally were not so expensive. But physicians have famously expensive taste.

Let's examine why that is with a thought experiment. Close your eyes for a moment and imagine a plastic surgeon. What do you picture? Does a man or woman in drab clothing driving a Toyota pop into your head? No! You likely imagine a well-manicured physician in a suit or dress driving a luxury car. I use a plastic surgeon in this example as one end of the "luxury doctor" extreme. But really, we imagine the same for all doctors. And we believe that the public, and our patients, do the same.

The result here is that we feel a pressure to live up to these imagined standards. The pressure feels real and external. However, in reality, it is internal and perceived. Regardless, this pressure compels us to use our high income to buy things we believe we want or need to live up to the Dr. Jones'. What's worse? We do so unintentionally. We rack up an expensive home, car, clothes, toys, and on and on. Usually, these items are paid for via financing that spread their cost into a "low" monthly payment. The problem is that these "low" payments add up. Suddenly, there isn't much of that income left over for creating a good margin. Suddenly, we must maintain our high income perhaps longer than we desired in order to cover all of these payments. Another vicious circle has begun due to this "doctor image."

Now, let's say that you have not made any of the previously discussed financial mistakes. You've created a healthy margin between what you make and what you spend. Unfortunately, this is not enough. And here enter the final financial faux pas of physicians. To build wealth and achieve financial freedom, we need to not only create a margin, we need to also grow that margin. We need our money to make money. The way to do this is by investing our hard earned and saved margin. However, investing seems complicated and risky. The reason we feel this way is yet again a lack of financial education among doctors. You actually can invest your money in a way that minimizing risk and maximizes your ability to reach your financial goals as I will show you. But this is not how it seems to us initially.

The fear and perceived risk of investing lead doctors to commonly make one of two critical mistakes. We either feel that investing is too risky and avoid it altogether. Or we feel that investing is too complicated for us, so we hire someone to do it for us. By avoiding investing all together, we completely fail to grow our margin, severely hindering our wealth building and prolonging our path to financial freedom.

By allowing someone else to manage our investing, we pay extra fees and taxes that drain our wealth and again prolong our path to financial well-being. Further, as high-income earners with little to no financial literacy, doctors are prime targets for financial predators. Committing to a financial relationship with such an advisor does far more damage than just subjecting you to increased fees and taxes. It's therefore necessary to at least know enough about personal finance to be able to tell a good advisor with a fair price from a bad one. However, as you will see in this book, one you know enough to do judge a financial advisor, you know enough to invest your own money.

Now that we have faced all of the common and costly financial mistakes that we make as physicians, we can put them in our past, where they belong. Now is the time to move forward, overcoming these mistakes and not allowing them to define us. In the next chapter, we will discuss how we can get started becoming a financially literate physician.

Chapter 3
Becoming a Financially Literate Physician

The majority of this book is action-oriented, focused on sharing the important "how-to's" of personal finance for physicians. However, before we get there, we first need to get philosophical. These next two chapters will help us to establish the right mindset and approach for our following actions aimed at getting us to financial well-being and freedom. Some of this mindset work may seem self-evident. But the importance of getting ourselves into the right frame of mind to create the financial life we deserve, and desire cannot be overstated. Lastly, these philosophical hurdles were not randomly selected. They represent the biggest hurdles that I experienced in the beginning of my journey as well as the most common struggles that others have confided in me as they began their journey.

The first stumbling block is always the one that seems the easiest: getting started. As we've gone over, personal finance can seem scary, intimidating, complex, and risky. Even though we know we just need to jump in and get started, it's all too easy to procrastinate and practice avoidance. Did I mention that the first personal finance book I ever read sat on my shelf for over a year before I read it? The misconception here is that we believe we must "feel ready" to get started. Doctors are perfectionists. We love to feel prepared and hate making mistakes. The reality however is that we will never feel ready to start and that we will make mistakes. And until we accept this, we will never start.

Think back to your first day on intern year. Did you feel ready? It's easy to convince ourselves now that we were up to the task at hand. But if you are anything like me, the honest answer is, "Hell no!" Now think back to any major achievement in your life. Were you ready or prepared when you began that journey? Chances are the answer is a resounding no. But you did start. And you succeeded. And that is the lesson. You have to start before you feel ready. In fact, you will *not* feel ready when you start any journey that is worthwhile. And your journey to becoming a better person and doctor through financial well-being is no different. That's why this chapter comes before the action-filled ones.

J. D. Frey, *Money Matters in Medicine*,
https://doi.org/10.1007/978-3-031-27300-1_3

The next philosophical leap of faith deals with the timing of this journey. In my experience in the physician finance space, anyone starting this journey feels that they are starting it too late. Universally, doctors tell me that they wish they started earlier and that they worry it is too late for them. Let me simple reassure you that it is not too late. And yes, that may be the only blanket statement made in this book! While the best day to start anything is always yesterday, the next best day is today.

I can assure you that I have seen physicians start this journey and successfully reach their goals in all phases of their career. In practicing medicine, we graduated from training with a bag of skills and tools. The way we help patients is by determining how best to use those skills and tools given the unique set of circumstances that a particular patient presents to us. Personal finance is no different. After reading this book, you will possess all the necessary financial skills and tools. You will then implement these strategies based on your own unique circumstances to successfully reach financial freedom. You would never deem a patient a "hopeless case." And neither should you do the same to yourself and your finances!

And while we are on the subject of timing, let's talk about time itself as a perceived barrier to financial well-being. One of my biggest concerns upon recognizing the contribution of my lack of financial well-being to my burnout was that I was just too busy to do anything about it. And I hear this echoed to me by others all the time. The truth is that, as doctors, we are all extremely busy. We have limited time outside of our clinical practice that rightfully is earmarked for family, friends, and personal wellness. So where does personal finance fit in?

Well, I will first point out that financial well-being is an important component of overall well-being as I have shared. So, your financial literacy is a worthy competitor for your time. But the reality remains, where can we fit all of this in? When I started my financial journey, I spent hours and hours studying, reading, listening, and testing out huge amounts of financial information. I quickly realized that this was not sustainable. So, what I did was focus instead on learning and creating small but powerful financial habits that fit into my life with minimal daily disturbance but maximum impact on my financial well-being.

It ultimately took me years of trial-and-error to figure these habits out. But it doesn't have to for you. This book breaks down everything that I have learned about, experimented with, failed at, and finally succeeded in the realm of physician finance. My goal is for you to be able to establish the same "high yield" financial habits that will allow you to focus less on your financial situation and more on your other priorities in life. And I aim to do this in as concise a format as possible so that even a doctor with the busiest clinical schedule can manage to read 5–10 pages of this book every day, setting the stage for massive financial action in as efficient a manner as possible.

And to do this, we are going to adhere strictly to the K.I.S.S. principle, keeping it simple. And that's not because there is a need to dumb down finances for our population of doctors. In fact, quite the opposite. Let's again use medicine as an example. We all know that, in medicine, there are simplifiers and complexifiers. Simplifiers can break down difficult medical concepts, presentations, and techniques to their component parts. Meanwhile, complexifiers take a medical topic and make it seem completely inaccessible. In my experience, simplifiers tend to be the ones who understand the concept at hand the best. So, I always seek out simplifiers in my field.

Personal finance is no different. There are simplifiers and complexifiers in personal finance. Unfortunately, unlike in medicine, complexifiers in personal finance may have an ulterior motive of making finance seem overly complex so that you determine the only way forward is to hire them to manage your money. On top of this, they may not actually fully understand the financial strategies that they are selling you themselves. As you will see throughout these chapters, personal finance is simple. So, find simplifiers and learn from them. In fact, if I am ever presented an investment that I don't understand, I am confident is determining that it is not a good investment.

Becoming financially well and literate is achievable for all physicians. Once we break down these philosophical and mindset barriers, we start to recognize the massive impact that financial freedom can have on our lives. Financial freedom - the ability to work and practice medicine because we want to, not because we have to – starts to take focus and become more tangible for us. But one hugely important task remains. Our path to financial well-being and freedom needs a purpose. And for that we need to answer the question, "Why?"

Chapter 4
What Is Your Why?

Throughout my life, I have been obsessed with accomplishment. Most of the time, it didn't matter what I was accomplishing. I sought any opportunity to achieve any reward, achievement, pat on the back, you name it. As over-achievers, I am sure many physicians can relate to this. The problem however is not seeking accomplishments. The problem is that I never stopped to think about why I wanted to accomplish these things. And this led to a string of arrival fallacies.

An arrival fallacy describes that feeling you get when you reach a goal, thinking it will lead to a profound change in internal happiness, only to find a fleeting sensation of fulfilment followed by an immediate need for more. When I was in college, I thought that once I made it to medical school, I would be happy. Then in medical school, I just had to reach residency. In residency, I just needed to publish a certain number of published papers or reach a certain number of accolades, and I would be happy. And finally, I determined that when I became an attending, I would be happy.

Again, none of these accomplishments are bad. But they never resulted in the effect that I thought they would. With each successive arrival fallacy, I travelled closer and closer to burnout. And I just could not figure out why. And therein lies the answer.

When we fail to establish why we are seeking some goal or purpose, the ultimate feeling we experience upon reaching it is emptiness. Continued hard work and self-sacrificing effort followed by a feeling of emptiness is a recipe for burnout. This is true in medicine but also for any other arena of your life, be it personal, professional, or anything in between. And this is also true of your journey to financial well-being and freedom.

Financial freedom is an immensely worthwhile goal. At a systems level, a nation of financially free physicians and healthcare workers would change healthcare for the better in ways we cannot even imagine. On a personal level, financial well-being makes us better doctors providing better care to our patients. However, if we don't first answer the question of *why* we are on this journey, the ultimate destination is emptiness. In fact, this can even lead to a worsening of burnout.

J. D. Frey, *Money Matters in Medicine*,
https://doi.org/10.1007/978-3-031-27300-1_4

Having a strong *why* for your journey to financial freedom is the most important step in the whole process of improving your financial well-being. I have unfortunately seen and spoken with too many physicians who are burned out or seeking to scale back in medicine seeking financial freedom without a strong *why*. They set their number to reach for financial freedom (we will talk about how to calculate this number coming up!) and work feverishly to reach it. But, when the do reach it, only another arrival fallacy greets them.

The reasons for this *why*-less arrival fallacy is that money is worthless. Taken by itself, money is simple a piece of paper or a set of "1's" and "0's" on your bank's server. Money only takes worth when we use it to create joy for ourselves, our loved ones, and the world at large. With this perspective, it's easy to envision why achieving a solely monetary goal breeds hollowness. This is where the adage "money can't buy happiness" comes from. When combined with a strong *why*, I argue that money can and does but not only happiness, but also time.

So, as you begin this journey, take the time necessary to sit by yourself or with your partner and loved ones. Think about *why* you want financial freedom. The following is the strong *why* that me and my wife, Selenid, created at the outset of our journey:

We want to gain financial well-being to enhance our overall well-being, to spend more time with our family and friends, and to pursue our passions (including medicine for me!) on our own terms.

You will determine why you want financial freedom unique to yourself. Your reasons will be your own and there are no wrong ones. Don't focus on creating it perfectly, instead focus on authenticity and being true to yourself. And then write it down as a list or a few sentences like ours.

Once you have your *why* created, you will use it to help propel you through your financial journey. How? The road to financial well-being and freedom is simple as we discussed previously. But that does not mean that it is easy. Like any worthwhile goal – eating healthier, exercising more, or quitting a vice – there will be challenges, temptations, and bumps in the road of this journey. There may even be times where you lose your path and forget why you are doing this in the first place.

And this is exactly the moment when your strong *why* springs into action! When times are good, you will be able to push yourself along your path. But in difficult times, it is your *why* that pulls you through the mud or over the bump in the road. Not infrequently, Selenid and I will review our *why* that you just read when we are having a tough time. That is why writing this down is so important. This is not a passing thought to establish and leave behind! Your *why* is on the journey with you.

In fact, your *why* is not just along for the ride. It is your purpose in pursuing this journey and goal in the first place! This purpose is what brings worth to the financial goals that you create for yourselves. So, that when you arrive at financial freedom, you don't discover another arrival fallacy but rather find the purpose, autonomy, and fulfilment you deserve.

With our strong *why* in hand, it's time to take action. And while our reflex may be to get offensive in our actions, the sports mantra that "defence wins championships" holds true in personal finance as well. We cannot increase our wealth or stably reach financial freedom without first ensuring we have the proper self-protection in place.

Chapter 5
Protecting Yourself Is the First Step

As physicians, especially at the beginning of our career, our future ability to practice medicine and earn money is our greatest asset. Therefore, the first step in building wealth is creating a stable foundation for it to sit upon. This involves protecting yourself and your future wealth from financial disaster. And proper insurance is what protects you from financial disaster. The trick, however, is to make sure that you only buy the insurance that you need.

There are two common problems that physicians encounter when it comes to protecting themselves through the insurance. And the incidence of both problems is about the same in my estimation. The first is having *not enough* insurance. And the second is having *too much* insurance.

Let's start with the problem of not enough insurance as this is maybe the more severe of the two. Insurance is something you buy that you hope you will never need to use. The best-case scenario with insurance is that you pay for nothing. Which is odd when you think about it. This is also why a lot of doctors question if and how much insurance they actually need. This is the main factor contributing to underinsured physicians.

When I started buying all the different types of insurance that I needed, it amazed me at how much it all added up to be. Especially as these are payments I'm making and hopefully never needing. It can feel like putting money down the drain. But it's not. And it's important to understand why doctors do need insurance as well as exactly what types they do (and don't) need. As stated above, having the correct insurance in place to protect you and your family in the case of financial catastrophe is extremely important.

On one end of the spectrum are these physicians feeling that insurance is too expensive to be worthwhile. And this brings us to our second problem of physicians being overinsured. Because on the other end of the spectrum are doctors looking to insure anything and everything because they feel any risk is too much. This is not the correct response either.

J. D. Frey, *Money Matters in Medicine*,
https://doi.org/10.1007/978-3-031-27300-1_5

For starters, you do not need insurance for items that, if broken, you should be able to cover out of pocket. This includes things like a cell phone, appliances, and the like. That is why we have an emergency fund (something we will cover in Chap. 7). These occurrences are inconveniences, not financial emergencies.

Moreover, there are a ton of salespeople out there who are willing to sell you a lot of insurance that you do not need and that can hamper your wealth building quite a bit. Every insurance product that doctors should have protects their future ability to practice and make money in one way or another. In fact, I think this is the best barometer and test to determine if you need an insurance product or not: Does this insurance protect my future ability to practice and make money? If yes, you probably need it. If no, then you don't.

So, what are these true financial emergencies that doctors need to protect themselves against and thus require insurance? The break down into 3 categories: risk of death, risk of disability, and risk of liability, both professional and personal. And four main categories of insurance exist to protect against these financial catastrophes: life insurance, disability insurance, malpractice insurance, umbrella insurance, and home/auto insurance.

Let's review these one by one so you can ensure you either already have or choose the right ways to protect yourself without being under- or over-insured.

Life Insurance

To start, life insurance is very important. Life insurance is insurance that will pay out to your loved ones (beneficiaries) if you pass away. Therefore, if you have anyone depending on your income like a spouse and /or kids among other possible dependents, you need life insurance.

And the type of life insurance that you need is called term life insurance. This is life insurance that covers you over a time period or term. If you die within that time period, the policy will pay out. The policy ends after the term is over.

Meanwhile, whole life insurance is the mother of all insurance products that doctors do not need but are all too often sold. Whole life insurance is a mixed investment and insurance product. It is a high commission product for insurance salespeople, so they have a huge conflict of interest and bias in selling it. The problem is that, especially in the early years of the policy, the premiums paid are not even worth the cash benefit for the policy. And while it is true that in later years, this relationship will inverse, the product buyer is almost always better off if they just invested that money wisely in broadly diversified, low-cost index funds as we will discuss later in this book.

The good news is that the term life insurance landscape is easy to navigate. It is a commodity. So, you just price out the options from various reputable companies and choose the cheapest one with the terms you want. I recommend working with an independent insurance broker who can shop you around to all the major companies to get you the best policy.

To apply, you will need your basic demographic information, a list of all medications, as well as a list of all doctors you currently see. Have this information ready to expediate the process. Once you apply, you will need to supply some information and generally take a physical. After this is done, they will grant you the policy.

Disability Insurance

Disability insurance is more complex but no less important. Again, I would recommend using an independent insurance broker to help with your disability policy. Remember, you don't pay extra for these brokers. They make their money from the companies whose products they use. By working with many companies (instead of one) in your best interest, they can get you the best product.

Disability insurance is insurance that you pay so that if you become disabled and cannot work anymore, the policy will pay you enough money such that you can keep living your life. It is much more expensive than life insurance but is completely necessary. Disability is a financial catastrophe. You need to protect yourself against it.

But how much disability insurance do you need? To find this out, calculate your monthly expense, minus tax because the policy payout is tax free generally. Also, try to calculate a budget that is a more shoestring budget. You need your policy to be able to cover at least this amount of monthly payment. Once you know how much insurance you need, decide on the delay after disability before the insurance policy pays out. You should have an emergency fund of 3–6 months expenses so you can reduce your premium by choosing a longer delay period.

Next, you need to figure out what terms and riders you want on the policy. First, your policy needs to be own-occupation. This means that if you are a surgeon and get hurt and can't perform the duties of your old job anymore, the policy still pays you. It still pays you even if you are able to work as an intensivist, let's say. This is important. Non-own occupation disability insurance will be cheaper. And that is for a reason. Because if you do get hurt and can't work in your usual job, but can work in another job, you won't get payments from the policy. And that defeats the whole purpose.

You also ideally will get a policy that is non-cancelable. This means that as long as you pay your premium, they cannot cancel your policy or raise your rates. Less ideal options are guaranteed renewable (they have to renew the policy but can raise the rates if they do so for all customers in your demographic category) and conditionally renewable (they can cancel the policy anytime they like).

In terms of disability insurance riders, you will generally want to include:

- Cost of living adjustment rider to keep your policy up with inflation
- Partial disability rider to cover some of your monthly costs if you become disabled, can work, but cannot make the same amount of money as before your disability
- A future increase option that allows you to increase the amount of coverage in the future for a commensurate increase in premium price

It is also possible to stack disability insurance policies with more than one company to increase your monthly payout. But this is only necessary if your monthly expenses are really that high.

Like life insurance, to apply, you will need your basic demographic information, a list of all medications, as well as a list of all doctors you currently see. Have this information ready to expediate the process. Once you apply, you will need to supply some information and generally take a physical. Once this is done, they will grant you the policy.

Lastly, I will note that some jobs offer group disability insurance. This is usually insurance that your employer has negotiated with a company that is not individualized to you. Some can be good, some not so good. You can supplement group with individual disability insurance. This is largely dependent on the product that your job offers. Speak with your HR representative to get details before speaking with a broker to get the most objective advice possible.

Malpractice Insurance

Malpractice insurance is expensive but a bit less complicated than disability insurance. In its purest sense, malpractice insurance protects you from professional liability. Therefore, if you are actively practicing medicine, you need malpractice insurance. And you want to make sure that your malpractice insurance carries high enough coverage. Generally, you want $1 million/$3 million in coverage. This means that the insurance policy will pay $1 million for each claim and up to $3 million in each policy year. The cost of suits can add up but having a decision made above these limits is also rare.

There are also two types of malpractice insurance.

The first, **claims-based malpractice insurance** determines who is responsible for paying based on when the claim was made. For example, if you worked at one hospital with one malpractice insurance in 2015 and now and you work in a different hospital and are sued by a patient from 2015, the old policy would not cover it. That is because they base things on when the claim is made. If you have this type of policy, you need to buy tail coverage for when you leave the job to cover claims made after you leave. It is expensive but not worth the risk not to have it.

The second type, occurrence-based coverage, is based on when the incident in question occurred. Therefore, in the above scenario, the old malpractice insurance would cover the claim since the occurrence was in 2015 when you had that insurance. Occurrence based in obviously better.

Many group policies will be available based on your job. Again, talk to your HR representative to get all details about the policy available to you. If they are not covering you at all or adequately enough, you will need to buy malpractice insurance on the market.

Now that we have covered protecting against professional liability, let's examine policies designed to protect us from personal liability.

Home/Auto Insurance

Thankfully, most doctors are used to paying home and auto insurance and do so without thinking. This is obviously necessary. Losing your home or automobile does constitute a financial emergency. Further, someone injuring themselves as a result of your automobile or home and seeking financial damages is a huge financial threat to your earning potential.

To find the right home and automobile insurance speak with an independent broker and price out many companies. Compare their prices and what they cover to determine what is best for you. They will often be able to bundle these policies for an overall lower rate. In general, it is worthwhile to have high deductibles on your plan to lower the premiums. You are a high-income earner and will have an emergency fund for unexpected things like a car accident with minor damage.

Umbrella Insurance

Umbrella insurance is insurance that covers any and every claim that could go against you and exceed your policy limits. It's like an umbrella in that way. For example, let's say that your car insurance has a bodily damage limit of $250,000 like mine. And you get in an accident. As a result, someone sues you for injuries for $500,000. If there was a successful judgement against me, my umbrella insurance would cover the extra $250,000.

Same with a home-based suit that exceeds your limits. It's relatively rare to have a suit against you that exceeds your policy limits. However, umbrella insurance is so inexpensive that I recommend getting it. Especially as you begin to accrue and grow your assets. Umbrella insurance usually can be obtained from the same insurance company/broker as your home and auto policy.

As a last note, umbrella insurance does not cover doctors above and beyond any malpractice decision in general. There are work based umbrella policies, but these are rare and generally much more expensive.

Now that we understand the insurance policies that will protect us and set the foundation for our wealth building, we are ready to start taking the steps towards building wealth. But, like any game, if we don't understand the rules, there is no way that we can play well and ultimately win. And, as we discussed earlier, common money misconceptions and taboos often cloud physicians' understanding of the game of financial well-being. But, once we know the rules, the path is clear and we can start effectively playing the game.

Chapter 6
Learn to Keep Score

No matter how simple a game is, if you don't know or understand the rules, you are bound to lose. In fact, you are probably more like to give up from frustration. That is how I felt before I began my financial education. Money and finance seemed like a black box, something that was too complex and intimidating to understand. But this was only because I, like so many doctors, lacked any financial education despite my long years of studying and never understood the rules.

And in personal finance and wealth building, the most important rule to understand is how to keep score. As we discussed in Chap. 2, there is a very common misconception about how wealth is scored. Most people believe that wealth is scored based on how much money we make or our income. Unfortunately, this is severely flawed. To build wealth, it does not matter how much money you make. It matters what you do with that money to build wealth. The doctor who makes $200,000 and saves 20% of that income has greater wealth than the doctor making $1,000,000 but saving 0% of it.

So, if income is not the scorecard of wealth, what is? And the answer is a measurement called net worth. Net worth is the measurement of your wealth. It is the rules of the game of personal finance. Understanding net worth therefore teaches you the rules of the game and lets you start playing…and winning.

What then, is net worth? In very simple terms, net worth is equal to your assets minus your liabilities. So then, what are assets and liabilities? Many definitions of assets and liabilities exist including some that are unnecessarily long and complicated. Simply put, assets are anything you own that put money in your pocket. This includes things like stock or bond investments and cash-flowing real estate.

© The Author(s), under exclusive license to Springer Nature
Switzerland AG 2023
J. D. Frey, *Money Matters in Medicine*,
https://doi.org/10.1007/978-3-031-27300-1_6

Conversely, liabilities are anything that takes money out of your pocket. The most common liabilities are debt and non-cash-flowing real estate like our primary homes.

$$\text{Net Worth} = \text{Assets}\left(\text{Put Money in your Pocket}\right)$$
$$- \text{Liabilities}\left(\text{Take Money Out of your Pocket}\right)$$

What is interesting to note in this calculation of net worth is that your income does not come into play. You will not find income listed anywhere on any net worth calculator. Why? Because income itself does nothing. Income can only help you buy assets or buy liabilities. This explains why a high income alone does not guarantee a high net worth. And how doctors making a lower income can be wealthier than their higher income colleagues. Again, it is not how much you make, but what you do with what you make that matters in the game of personal finance and wealth. Those are the rules!

Now that we understand what net worth is and that it, rather than income, is the measurement of wealth, let's discuss how to calculate your own net worth. Essentially, you will just use the equation above. On a sheet of paper, list all of your assets in one column and add them up. In another column, list all of your liabilities and add them up as well. Now, subtract your liabilities from your assets and you have your net worth (Fig. 6.1). You can also look up any net worth calculator online to do this as well—they are all largely the same and equally effective!

When I calculated and looked at my net worth for the first time, it was around - $500,000! I obviously did not like that it was so heavily in the negative. However, the fear I worried I would feel upon seeing my net worth (I had guessed it was going to be pretty low!) never materialized. Instead, I felt empowered. And more on that in a moment. The point is that you may not like the number that you see. You likely will want it to be higher. And that is okay. Financial well-being is not about what number your net worth is currently. It is about creating a plan and starting the journey towards your goal net worth and financial freedom.

And that is why I felt so empowered when I saw my negative net worth for the first time. Because after I calculated it, I could study it. I could look at the asset column and discern what I could do to increase this column. And I could look at the liabilities column and develop plans to minimize and limit this column. Now that I knew the rules of the game, I could finally start playing! I no longer needed to flail about in the dark or just hope that someday this would magically take care of itself. Now, the power was in my hands!

And with this newfound grasp on the rules and subsequent financial empowerment, I now began to understand the steps I could take to increase my net worth and progress down the path to financial freedom. But there was still one problem. To increase my assets and decrease my liabilities, I needed money. And, despite having a good income, I never seemed to have any money. This needed to change.

Fig. 6.1 Example net
worth calculation for an
early career physician.
Note that income is not
listed anywhere!

Assets	
Home Market Value	$400,000
401k	$100,000
Roth IRA	$10,000
Taxable Investment Account	$10,000
Savings	$30,000
Real Estate Value	$150,000
Total Assets	$700,000
Liabilities	
Student Debt	$250,000
Home Mortgage	$350,000
Credit Card Debt	$15,000
Car Loans	$25,000
Total Liabilities	$640,000
Net Worth	$60,000

Chapter 7
Harvesting Net Worth from our Income Starts with a Budget

When I ask physicians who are living pay check to pay check what they are doing to build their net worth, they often respond that they just don't have the money to do anything about it. While this may be how it feels for them (it certainly did for me!), it is not reality. We have money via our high doctor income. But we are not using it correctly. Instead of harvesting that money to grow our net worth, we let it evaporate from our hands via monthly expenses on goods and services, some of which are necessary and some of which are not.

We have established *what* net worth is. But, before moving on, it's important that we address the *how* of net worth. So, what is the formula to grow our net worth and build wealth? It's simple. To build wealth, we need to create and grow our margin.

$$\text{Building Wealth} = \text{Creating} + \text{Growing Our Margin}$$

And our margin is equal to what we make minus what we spend (Fig. 7.1). Much of this book will discuss the second part of this equation, growing our margin via investing. However, we cannot successfully invest our margin if we never create it in the first place. And this is where most physicians get held up.

How then can we create a margin to start building wealth? The answer is right in the definition of the margin itself. To create a margin, we can either increase the money coming in or decrease the money going out of our lives. We are in control of both of these variables. While we will talk about increasing what we make in Chap. 13, all of us are in much greater control of the "what we spend" portion of this wealth-building equation. In fact, what we spend is 100% in our control at all times. It therefore becomes the first aspect of our personal finances that we need to address in our path to financial well-being.

Luckily, there is a readily available tool to help us tilt this wealth building margin in our favour. And that tool is a budget. Now, if you are like most people including myself, your initial reaction to reading about budgets may be to roll your eyes in disgust. I get it. But stick with me.

J. D. Frey, *Money Matters in Medicine*, https://doi.org/10.1007/978-3-031-27300-1_7

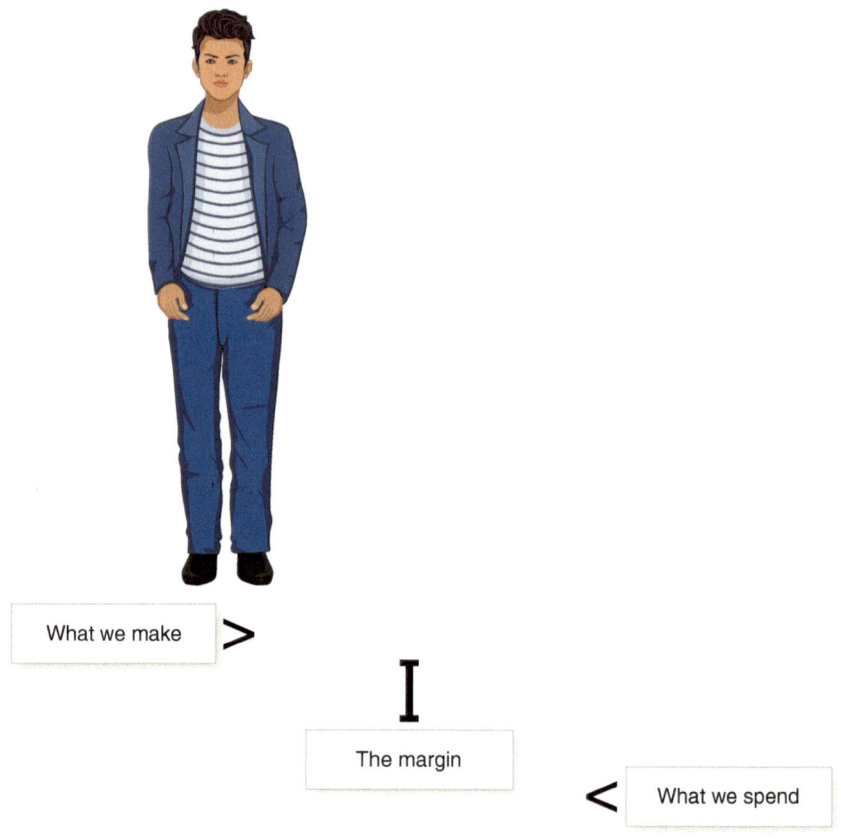

Fig. 7.1 Creating a margin

Most people really hate budgets. At first glance, they appear to be these restrictive set of spending rules designed to torture you. Doctors even carry more general vitriol for budgets due to their years of delayed gratification with limited spending power in training. This is exactly how I felt about them.

But once I learned the rules and formulas of the wealth building game, my mindset about budgets completely shifted. Let's dig into that and I feel confident you will experience a similar shift. Budgets are not restrictive. In fact, they are permissive. Budgets are tools that help guide you on your path to financial freedom. My budget tells me how much I can spend on various categories of expenses while still creating a big enough margin that I can then grow to reach my financial goals and achieve financial freedom. A budget allows you to harvest your income to create a margin and build wealth. In that way, my budget is like a treasure map. And no pirate ever hated a treasure map! Armed with this new perspective, I started to look forward to my monthly budget review session with my wife.

Budgeting also helps us to develop one of the most important financial habits for wealth-building: paying ourselves first. If you are like I was, when you received your pay check, you paid everyone else in your life first. You paid your mortgage or rent, utilities, groceries, and all other expenses. Then you kept whatever was left over for yourself. The problem with this pay yourself last approach is that we usually end up with nothing left over for ourselves at the end. In fact, all too often we spend more than we made and end the month with new credit card debt. This is not conducive to creating a margin to build wealth.

We want to create a new paradigm wherein we pay ourselves first whenever we receive income. When a pay check comes in, we save a portion for ourselves. Then we pay the other people in our lives with what remains. Now, I am not saying that you should not pay your bills or financial commitments. That is not what paying yourself first is about. Instead, paying yourself first teaches you to prioritize the other people that you are paying in your life. If I ask anyone whether a stranger should pay themselves or someone else, they always answer the same way. It's time we start practicing what we preach!

Next, we must consider just how much we should pay ourselves each month. Put another way, how big of a margin or savings rate do we need? There is no set answer, but a good rule of thumb is to create a margin of at least 20% of your gross (pre-tax) pay. That is how you harvest your income to begin building wealth. Now, this is not to say that you need to have a savings rate of 20% on the first budget that you run. But a minimum of 20% is your goal. In fact, if all you do after reading this book is create a 20% savings rate and invest it in the manner that I will share in the upcoming chapters, I can assure that you will reach financial freedom on your terms.

Just saying we need a 20% savings rate is one thing. But we need to put it into practice. Your budget is the tool that will take this margin creation from abstract to reality. Before I describe the process through which you will create your budget, let me again reiterate that your goal is not to build this margin of 20% on the first go-round. If you can, great! But if not, that's just fine.

When my wife and I created and ran our first budget while still in training, our savings rate was 0%. Our goal became to increase it by 1% each month. Now that I am an attending, our savings rate is 40–50% each month! This is also a great strategy for any attending physicians will expenses matching their income and impeding their margin creation. It is not realistic to expect to cut these expenses down to a 20% savings rate in one fell swoop. Little by little, use your budget to pare these expenses until you are at your goal savings rate. This is about creating the habits and routines that will serve your wealth-building throughout your life.

Let's now go through the steps to create and implement your budget so you can begin growing your savings rate and building your wealth.

Creating your Simple Budget

- Come up with a list of broad categories of expenses (i.e. rent/mortgage, groceries, entertainment, taxes – don't forget taxes, etc.)

    - Do NOT make one category "Amazon." You need to break out what exactly you are buying at Amazon to avoid this becoming a black box.

- Label each expense category as a *need* or a *want*
- Go to your bank account(s)/credit card(s) and put every single expense from the past month (first of the month to first of the month) in an expense category
- Add up the total for each expense category
- Add up the grand total for the month and make sure it is less (or at worst equal to) your monthly income
- Do you have enough left over to save for your financial goals?

    - If yes, great! If no, what can you adjust to make this happen?
    - Aim for a savings rate of at least 20%

- Now, go through each category and decide how much you can spend in the future while still reaching your goals

Now you have your own budget and a treasure map to build your wealth. This should realistically take approximately 30–45 minutes. I will also note that if you have a partner, you must do this together. It simply will not work if one of you tries to do it alone. With our budget guide in hand, we now need to implement and check it every month.

Implementing your Simple Budget

Take 1 full month before reviewing your budget again. Then,

- Set aside 30 minutes in the evening of the first of every month
- Sit with your Excel budget sheet open (or whatever budget program/piece of paper you use)
- Go through each expense from that month (checking accounts, savings withdrawals, credit purchases)
- Tabulate and total them in the appropriate *needs* or *wants* expense category
- Calculate how much above or below you are in each expense category
- Calculate how much above or below you are in total for the month
- If you saved more than expected, put it towards debt pay down, investing, or reward yourself!

It will likely take a month or two to get the "feel" of how much you can spend in each category. Don't get frustrated if you are over by a bit in some categories at first. This will happen and happens to me still. This exercise is all about creating a life-long habit for financial success, not achieving perfection right away.

And that is the point. Because this type of budget is a permissive budget, not a restrictive budget. This may appear to be simply semantics. However, as discussed earlier, the way that we perceive our budget has a huge impact on our relationship with it. With a permissive budget like the one we are creating, there will be months when we are over-budget in some categories. And that is alright. Because other months we will be under-budget in those same or other categories.

In fact, I recommend building some permissive wiggle room right into your budget. In our budget,[1] we have a category labelled "fudge factor." Its purpose is right in the name. If we buy some non-categorized item or service, it goes into our "fudge factor" for the month. If we don't use it during a certain month, that allotted "fudge factor" money simply adds on top of our savings rate. Compare this with the traditional restrictive budget and you can see why a permissive one is not just tolerable, but dare I say fun.

At this point, you are armed not only with an understanding of the rules to the wealth building game. You are also armed with the means to create the savings rate that will let you start playing the game. So, what are the first steps?

---

[1]You may find our budget template to create your own at: https://prudentplasticsurgeon.com/budgeting-made-simple/

Chapter 8
Dealing with our Biggest Liabilities

Let's think back to the rules of wealth building. Our goals are twofold: to increase our assets and to decrease our liabilities. But which do we begin with? You may have guessed from the title of this chapter but our first step in the path to financial freedom is reducing and eliminating our liabilities. This may not seem obvious.

Does this mean that you need to have zero liabilities before you start adding to the asset column? No, it doesn't. But it does mean that you need to prioritize and have an accelerated plan for managing and eliminating liabilities. That is what this chapter will teach you to do.

But first, let's dig deeper into the argument of whether it is better to initially pay off debt (eliminate liabilities) or invest (build assets). Since we know the rules of the game, we know that if our goal is to build wealth, we want to increase our net worth – the measurement of wealth. However, a liability is anything that takes money out of your pocket and is the main detractor of our net worth. Therefore, by eliminating things that take money out of your pocket, more money stays inside your pocket that can be used to build wealth. But, if we instead try to increase assets without eliminating liabilities, it is like trying to fill a bucket with a hole in it. Using another analogy, the first step when you have dug yourself a hole (i.e., with debt), is to climb out. Only then can you begin to walk and run to our financial goals.

In fact, as we examine our net worth calculation closely, we see that for every $1 of debt that is avoided or eliminated, our net worth increases by exactly $1. Few to no other investments or assets will have this immediate, one-to-one return. Extending this even further, paying off debt has a guaranteed return, something that no other investment can tout. If you pay off a debt with a 7% interest rate, you just received an immediate 7% return on that money. No matter what anyone else tells you, no investment except paying off your debt is guaranteed. We simply can't ignore a guaranteed strategy to grow our net worth immediately with our newly established savings rate.

There will be some who cite something called *interest arbitrage* as a justification for ignoring their liabilities. The argument goes that if one can invest their money

J. D. Frey, *Money Matters in Medicine*,
https://doi.org/10.1007/978-3-031-27300-1_8

by building assets for a higher return than they would receive by paying off their liabilities, one should prioritize those assets over the liabilities. Put more simply, if you can invest your money for a 7% return, why pay off a debt with 5% interest? And I can't argue with that. The math is not on my side.

But building wealth is not just about math. It is also about behaviours and habits. And interest arbitrage has some pretty serious flaws, both in terms of math and behaviour. We've already talked about one of these. No investment is guaranteed. As we will discuss later, investing in the overall stock market for the long term is the safest way to invest. And over history, these yearly returns have averaged 7%. But is this 7% return guaranteed? No way! So, if your interest arbitrage strategy is based on a guaranteed return (and it usually is), this strategy is flawed.

Further, our human behaviour gets in the way of our best-intentioned plans—in life and in finance. We can tell ourselves that our savings rate—our margin—will go towards this asset or that asset all we want. All too often, however, extra money that may be earmarked for investing goes not towards wealth building, but towards some other expense. This is human nature. Paying off debt short-circuits this natural tendency. Put your debt payments on autopay to eliminate this common pitfall.

My last argument in favour of liability elimination as our starting point for wealth building is simple and anecdotal. But that doesn't take away its power. I have yet to meet anyone who has paid off their debts and eliminated their liabilities who regrets it!

With that put to bed, let's talk about using our savings rate to manage and eliminate our liabilities and debt. First, we must acknowledge that there are two types of liabilities. These are present liabilities and future liabilities. First, we need to manage future liabilities. And the best way to do this is to eliminate them completely. That is why the first step is to establish an emergency fund.

An emergency fund consists of 3–6 months' worth of expenses kept in a savings account or money market fund. This fund is designed to be there in case of, you guessed it, emergency. You may recall in Chap. 5 that doctors do not need insurance for items that that they can replace with cash. Your emergency fund is where that cash comes from. By having this money in place in case of emergency, you avoid the need to take on more debt to cover these unexpected expenses.

Even more, your emergency fund protects you if something unexpected happens to your income. For a long time, physicians believed that their income was guaranteed. Unfortunately, the COVID-19 pandemic proved this to be a fallacy. With your emergency fund ready, you have at least 3–6 months' worth of expenses covered even in the unlikely event that your income went goes to zero.

Two common questions surrounding emergency funds are where the money should be kept and how much money is the right amount. The first question has a very concrete answer while the second is more personal. Emergency funds should be maintained in either a high-yield savings account or a money market fund. These funds exist for emergencies, which you inherently cannot predict ahead of time. Therefore, your goal with this money is not growth but rather security and availability. Imagine needing a large sum for an emergency but your money is invested in the stock market during a downturn. Suddenly your 3–6 months' worth of expenses has dropped to 1 month's expenses. Now you have another emergency.

In terms of how much money is the right amount for your emergency fund, there is no right or wrong answer. It will all depend on your circumstances and risk tolerance. I do recommend 3–6 months of expenses as a minimum. However, if you have a lower risk tolerance, 12 months may feel more secure to you. If you have multiple streams of unrelated income, perhaps an emergency fund closer to the 3 months end of the spectrum strikes the right balance.

To create your emergency fund, simply add up your monthly expenses. This will be easy since you already have your budget! Then, determine how many months' worth of expenses you want in your emergency fund. That becomes your target. Open a high-yield savings account with your bank or a money market fund with your brokerage and start using your monthly savings rate to preferentially fill this emergency fund to your goal.

After planning to avoid future liabilities, it's time to attack your present liabilities. For most physicians, the biggest items in the liability column will be your student debt and home mortgage. Creating a paydown plan places the locus of control of our debt back in our hands. And the goal of this plan will be to pay off our debt as quickly and efficiently as possible.

I once overheard one doctor telling another that they planned to die with their student loans. This way, the loans would be discharged upon their death. In their mind, this was winning. Because they never fully paid off their lender. The reality however could not be further from the truth. When you are a lender, your ideal scenario is that your borrower never pays you back fully. That way, you just keep collecting more and more interest over time. If you really want to stick it to your lender, pay off your debt aggressively and ahead of schedule. That way you pay back as little interest as possible. That's how you win! Don't be fooled by small monthly payments that add up and slowly eat away at your financial freedom. Before you know it, you may be working because you have to, not because you want to. Thankfully our debt payoff plan will be designed for us to win this battle.

To create your debt payoff plan, I recommend using what is called the snowball method. The first step will be to gather all your debts and write them each out on a sheet of paper of Excel spreadsheet. This will include student loans, mortgages, car loans, credit card debt, and the like. Once you have gathered all your loans, the next step is to arrange them in one of two orders. You can order them from lowest amount to greatest amount or from highest interest rate to lowest interest rate. Either of these strategies work just fine, it is up to your preference.

Now that you have your debts ordered, it's time to start paying them off! With the money that you have allocated towards your debt payment in your budget, make minimum required payments on all your loans. Put whatever amount is leftover after these minimum payments towards the first loan on your list. Keep doing that until the first loan is totally paid off. Then move on to the second loan. And then the third loan. And on and on.

The reason this is called the snowball method is because each loan that is paid off no longer requires a monthly minimum payment. Now, that amount can be added on to pay off the next loan in line. As more loans are paid off, the snowball of money paying off subsequent loans grows. This is exactly how I am paying off my loans!

The next logical question is how much of our monthly savings rate should be put towards paying off debt? The answer is to allocate enough towards debt payments such that you can be debt free in 5–10 years. Remember, the sooner you pay off debt, the greater your monthly cash flow becomes and the more your path toward asset building and financial freedom is accelerated. Since we know the rules, we should play to win. In my case, my wife and I allocate approximately 1/3 of our monthly savings rate towards debt paydown. This will allow us to pay off all student debt in 5 years.

The snowball method provides a general guideline for everyone to create their own debt paydown plan. However, individual factors will influence your exact personalized design. Your level of indebtedness will obviously impact how much you need to allocate to loans each month from your savings rate. The type of student loans that you have—private or federal student loans—will also play a role.

Private loans are just like a mortgage or car loan or credit card debt. There are no federal protections. Therefore, the best strategy for these loans is to pay them off aggressively based on the snowball method. If an opportunity comes to refinance these loans through another loan company for a lower interest rate, take advantage!

On the flip side, federal loans require some additional planning. The main consideration is whether you are or will be pursuing Public Service Loan Forgiveness (PSLF). PSLF is a government program for physicians in which doctors who make income-based payments on their loans and work at a qualifying non-profit institution (like public or most academic hospitals) have their remaining qualifying government loans forgiven after 10 years. This is obviously a huge advantage for anyone who can use this program.

Therefore, if you have federal loans that qualify for PSLF (most do but check with your loan servicer), you need to determine if you will pursue this program which will influence your debt paydown plan. Here are some general rules of thumb:

- If you do not or do not plan to work for a qualifying non-profit institution, then you will create your plan without considering PSLF. Simply pay off your federal loans based on the Snowball method and take advantage of any refinancing opportunities similar to private loans.
- If you are in training and have a long training period (>5 years), taking advantage of PSLF usually makes sense. Shorter training periods mean that income-based repayments will increase once you become an attending and minimize future forgiveness.
- If you have a low income to debt ratio, PSLF is generally advantageous. Those with higher income to debt ratios are usually better served paying off the loans aggressively as higher income-based payments leave little room for significant future forgiveness.
- Lastly, if you do plan to pursue PSLF, do *not* refinance your loans. Refinancing your loans essentially turns them into private loans. Your ability to utilize PSLF is eliminated the moment your federal loans are refinanced.

The other biggest potential liability for doctors is their primary home. Remember, a primary home is a liability because it takes money *out* of your pocket. It does not put money in your pocket. And relying on your home to experience positive market appreciation is akin to speculation, not investing. Therefore, the decision to rent or mortgage your first home as a doctor, or any high-income earner, is a sticky one.

It's a decision that is quite emotional and can have long-lasting impact on your wealth-building. It's also very controversial. But first, please note that I am referring to the decision to mortgage or rent your first primary residence AFTER training i.e., as an attending. The reasons for a trainee to buy are few and far between. Perhaps if you are house-hacking or will be training in one location for 7 or more years. But really, renting is better as a trainee. With that disclaimer in place, what is a fresh residency/fellowship grad with an 8x pay increase to do after decades of delayed gratification?

Do you mortgage or rent your first home? The generalizable advice is in favor of for renting your first home. There are strong reasons for this. First, you are starting a new job that you may hate and want to leave after a year or so. It is not an insignificant percentage of doctors that leave their first job within 5 years and relocate. If this happens to you, and it might, selling your house is the last thing that you will want to deal with. If your local market has been cold since you bought your home, you may be selling for less than you bought. Even if you sell at the same price that you bought, you will lose money via the closing and selling costs that you must pay.

Even worse, if you can't find a buyer, you now must pay for two homes. Sure, you can try to rent this house to cover your mortgage and associated expenses. The bad news with this strategy is that rents for single family homes in A-class neighborhoods rarely cover the expenses, let alone cash flow. Being a reluctant landlord is never a good situation. If you are renting, all these issues disappear. In most cases, you can just leave when your lease ends with no issue. At worst, you break your lease early and move with all strings cut.

Renting also allows you to ease into your new paycheck. As a metaphor, I've never received a windfall in my life. No inheritances, lottery wins, or any such event. If I ever do though, I know exactly what we are going to do with it. We're not going to buy a fancy car, new home, or some other toy. I'm not even going to use it to pay back my loans immediately. It's going to sit in an account for at least a month, probably more like 3 months. This way, I'll acclimate to it and not spend it emotionally. Here's to hoping we all have such problems!

Managing your first paycheck follows a similar philosophy in my mind. Renting your first home allows one to acclimate to their new paycheck without spending emotionally. Spending emotionally can often lead to spending regret as expenses add up and you don't have as much to save or invest as you would want. Or maybe you don't have anything left to save or invest—you're back to living paycheck to paycheck. This is what we want to avoid.

The most compelling reason to rent instead of mortgaging your first home is to save money to pay off debt and invest. The mortgage is just the beginning of the payments when you buy a house. The main expenses people talk about are PITI—Principal, Interest, Taxes, and Insurance. But there are also usual wear and tear repairs as well as unexpected issues that arise. Buy a house without furniture and you may be enticed to buy all new furniture. (Better in my opinion to leave rooms unfurnished that to buy a bunch of expensive furniture that you won't use all that often.)

These payments tend to surprise new doctors who often just compare their current rent to the principal + interest payments of a prospective house. This is comparing apples to oranges. Suddenly, you may be shifting money earmarked for your debt payments or your retirement plan to support your home purchase. Don't sacrifice your future financial freedom for a house. You will be able to find beautiful places to live without needing to do this, even in higher cost of living areas.

Therefore, as mentioned above, the overall recommendation for new physician grads becoming an attending is to rent, not buy your first home.

However, I didn't follow my own advice. And the reason that my wife and I bought our first home is multifold. But the bottom line is that we set a budget of what we could afford, created criteria for what we were looking for, and kept emotion out of it as much as possible.

First, we had created our written financial plan and budget before buying our home (like you are learning to do by reading this book!). A written financial plan and budget MUST come first. The first things we factored into our budget were our "needs" and our savings, including loan payments. Once we set this number with a savings rate of 41%, we knew how much we would have for everything else, including PITI and other expenses for a mortgage.

And yes, you can use some rules of thumb in making sure you don't buy too much house. The purchase price should be less than 2x your annual income (ours is 1.2× our salary). Your annual mortgage to income ratio should be less than 28%. These generalities are fine. However, I recommend setting a budget and knowing down to the dollar how much house you can buy. You'll feel a lot more confident and relaxed in your decision.

Second, we set strict criteria for our home. Much like with an investment property, we set criteria for the type of home that we were looking for. If a house didn't meet these criteria, it wasn't for us. Most home buyers let emotion dictate which houses they consider and like. We set these hard terms to limit the effect of emotion in our decision.

Our main criteria were that the home:

- Be below our maximum purchase price (2× our income would be over $1 million but we set a maximum sticker of $700,000)
- Have 4 bedrooms minimum (enough for 1 more kid at least)
- Be in our preferred school district
- Be in our preferred town with lower taxes than surrounding areas
- Have a finished basement
- Have a fenced backyard to keep our kids and dogs contained
- Have room for potential expansion in future
- And that we would use a physician loan requiring 0% down

By following these criteria, we were selecting for a home that we knew we would want to stay for at least 10 years. As I've said before, the housing market is like the stock market – volatile in the short term but stably increasing in the long term. Buying a home that we were planning to live long-term, we maximized our chances of making a profit when we sold. Also, by using a physician loan with 0% down, we would not need to sacrifice any savings or investments. My wife and I agreed that if we didn't find a house that fit these criteria, we would rent until we did.

Most Importantly, I Moved Home. This is probably the biggest qualifier of our decision to mortgage or rent a house. We were moving back to my hometown of Buffalo, NY. My wife is from Miami but she has lived in Western New York for 8 years of her life and spent a ton of time in Buffalo during our 11 years together.

Further, I had vetted my job for a long time prior to making the decision to take it. This included time in the hospital, with the partners, with the partners spouses and my spouse. I knew the job inside and outside by speaking with the partners obviously, the hospital administration including the COO, and former residents who spent time with the department. It has been an amazing fit and I am not surprised. I knew and wanted exactly what I was getting into. Both factors minimized the risk of me becoming a reluctant landlord or a reluctant double mortgage payer.

In the end, we found a house that met our criteria and beyond. It was below our maximum purchase price. The house was initially listed for $730,000, above our limit. We had our eye on it for a while and then 1 day, the seller dropped the list price to $699,000. We made a trip to go see it in person about a week after this. The home had four bedrooms, a fenced backyard, was in our school district and town of choosing, had a finished basement, and plenty of room to expand if we desired in the future. We offered $675,000 with all furniture and the playground included. The offer was accepted. Buying in this case made sense.

So, rent or buy? As I've shown, there is no simple answer to this question. If I could only give one simple answer, it would be that you should rent until you are stable at your job and have a significant savings rate for debt pay down and investments. However, there are scenarios where buying your first property can also accommodate these parameters as in my situation. Before making any decision, you first have to establish your financial foundation and create a plan. And you are taking great strides in doing this just by reading this book!

With these rules of thumb in mind, it is important to look over your individual circumstances to determine the best plan. But regardless, remember that your unique plan needs to allow you to be debt-free except mortgage in 5–10 years and mortgage-free by the time you retire. Because once your liabilities are managed, you can finally start building your assets. And your assets will pave the road to your financial freedom. However, before we can start off on this road, we must have a destination in mind. So, how can we figure out how much money we need to be financially free as well as how to get it?

Chapter 9
Securing Your Nest Egg in Five Steps

We all have a goal number to reach for financial freedom. A magical number that, once we reach it in assets and investments, allows us to work because we want to, not because we have to. Or even to not work at all. After all, that is the freedom part of financial freedom. And each of our numbers will be unique to us individually. However, before learning how to build our assets and investments, we need to know what the goal for them is. This will obviously impact how we craft our financial plan.

How then can we determine the goal for our nest egg and financial freedom? This chapter will teach you the five steps to do exactly this. You can also download a calculator to help you with these steps at www.prudentplasticsugeon.com.

Step 1

The first step in the retirement calculator for doctors is figuring out your monthly expenses. To do this, sit with the budget that you have created. Go through your expenses and think about how these will change in retirement (Fig. 9.1).

For example, you will need to make sure you include:

- Healthcare if not Medicare age
- School expenses if kids are not yet through their education
- Long term care costs
- Vacations

Some examples of things you will no longer need include:

- Life insurance
- Disability insurance
- Student loans
- Consumer debt

© The Author(s), under exclusive license to Springer Nature
Switzerland AG 2023
J. D. Frey, *Money Matters in Medicine*,
https://doi.org/10.1007/978-3-031-27300-1_9

Step 1 - How much retirement savings will you need?	
What do you estimate your monthly expenses in retirement to be?	10,000
How much annual "salary" do you want in retirement?	120,000
Nest egg required	3000000
Step 2 - How much annually do you need to save to reach your goal?	
Annual estimated savings amount	76,668
Current Savings/Investments	80,000
Expected rate of return (5% conservatively)	5%
Years until goal retirement (Goal retirement age - Current age)	25
Estimated Nest egg under above conditions	$3,930,049.61
Estimated annual savings required to achieve this nest egg	76,668

Fig. 9.1 The first step in your estimated retirement calculator is to determine your expected monthly expenses in retirement

- Hopefully your mortgage since you will have paid this off as part of your debt paydown plan!

I recommend always overestimating how much you want/need.

Step 2

This step is quite simple. Just multiply your monthly expenses from Step 1 by 12 to calculate your annual estimated expenses in retirement.

Step 3

Once you know how much money you want/need to have in retirement on a yearly basis, you can figure out the nest egg you will need to achieve that. It's a simple equation based on the 4% rule. The 4% rule is a general rule of thumb based on a famous economic study called the Trinity study. The Trinity study which showed that you can safely withdraw 4% of your investment nest egg each year in retirement and have a very high chance of not running out of savings before you die.

Step 1 - How much retirement savings will you need?	
What do you estimate your monthly expenses in retirement to be?	10,000
How much annual "salary" do you want in retirement?	120,000
Nest egg required	3000000
Step 2 - How much annually do you need to save to reach your goal?	
Annual estimated savings amount	76,668
Current Savings/Investments	80,000
Expected rate of return (5% conservatively)	5%
Years until goal retirement (Goal retirement age - Current age)	25
Estimated Nest egg under above conditions	$3,930,049.61
Estimated annual savings required to achieve this nest egg	76,668

Fig. 9.2 By dividing your estimated annual retirement expenses by 4% (or multiplying by 25), you can estimate the nest egg you will require

It is important to note here that the 4% rule is only a rule of thumb. Some more recent studies suggest a more appropriate withdrawal rate would be 3.5%. However, for our purposes in developing a goal nest egg, the 4% rule serves its purpose well. We are looking for a guidepost. It is by no means perfect. But it's a great way to make these estimates.

However, if you are more conservative, you can certainly use a lower withdrawal rate for your calculations. I would not recommend using a larger withdrawal rate. As mentioned above, it's always better to be conservative and underestimate.

Regardless, to determine your goal nest egg, you will simply divide your estimated annual expenses by your withdrawal rate. Using the 4% rule, this means dividing your yearly desired retirement expenses by 4% (or multiplying by 25). This number now represents the nest egg required to sustain your retirement (Fig. 9.2).

But we can't stop here after only three steps. Even though we have our goal nest egg number, we still need help figuring out how to put this nest egg together!

Step 4

Remember, the key to achieving financial freedom is simple. We know the rules and the formula: Increase the difference between what you make and what you spend. This is your "margin." Then you need to invest this margin (which we will cover in the next chapter).

So, to reach your retirement nest egg you need to figure out four main variables.

1. How much you need to save each year,
2. How much you already have saved,
3. How long you have until you plan to retire, and
4. Your expected rate of return on your savings

These four variables will largely determine the nest egg that you retire with. The great thing is that they are relatively in your control, especially the first three factors.

For this step, you will need to either download my retirement calculator from www.prudentplasticsurgeon.com or open an Excel spreadsheet. We will then use either of these tools to enter the data for the four factors above and calculate our necessary savings to reach our goal nest egg.

First, enter your current savings amount and how long you plan to work until you retire (again, this is an estimate). Next, enter your expected *after tax, after fees* return on your investments. Be conservative. Better to underestimate and have more later than vice versa. As we will discuss in the next chapter, a good estimate is 7% for expected rate of return although you will see that I have been more conservative and used 5%.

Next, enter your expected annual savings amount from your budget. If you are using the calculator, you will automatically generate the expected nest egg grown based on the four factors that you entered. If you are using your own spreadsheet, use the formula (Fig. 9.3):

Step 1 - How much retirement savings will you need?	
What do you estimate your monthly expenses in retirement to be?	10,000
How much annual "salary" do you want in retirement?	120,000
Nest egg required	3000000
Step 2 - How much annually do you need to save to reach your goal?	
Annual estimated savings amount	76,668
Current Savings/Investments	80,000
Expected rate of return (5% conservatively)	5%
Years until goal retirement (Goal retirement age - Current age)	25
Estimated Nest egg under above conditions	$3,930,049.61
Estimated annual savings required to achieve this nest egg	76,668

Fig. 9.3 Inputting your current variables into the retirement calculator will predict your expected nest under current conditions to compared with your required next egg estimated in Step 3

$$= FV\left(\begin{array}{l}[\text{Expected Rate of Return}],[\text{Years to Retirement}], \\ -[\text{Annual Savings}], -B[\text{Current Savings}],0\end{array}\right)$$

Now that you see the estimated nest egg generated under these conditions, you can compare it with your goal nest egg. Is it enough? If so, then you know that you are saving enough money to invest to reach your goal nest egg. If not, play around with the variables. While there is not much you can do from your current savings and expected rate of return and you likely will not want to unnecessarily extend the length of your working years, you can adjust your annual savings. That is 100% in your control now that you have a budget in place.

Adjust your annual savings rate until you estimated nest egg is equal to or greater than your goal nest egg. If necessary, go back to readjust your budget so that you raise or lower your savings rate to meet that necessary to reach this goal nest egg.

As a note here, this calculation does not directly factor sin forms of passive income that can sustain you during retirement. This includes things like rental income or dividends. What Selenid and I do is subtract that expected yearly total of passive income from our expected yearly expenses. Then we calculate the savings needed to reach a now amended nest egg based on the amended yearly savings.

For example, let's say we expect to have yearly expenses of $200,000. But we also have rental income from a cash-flowing real estate property of $100,000/year. Then, we would only need to cover $100,000 ($200,000–$100,000) in annual expenses. This equals a nest egg of roughly $2.5 million compared to compared to $5.1 million without the rental income.

Step 5

This is the most important step. I have seen and know so many people who will spend hours and hours running these calculations. But then they don't change their spending habits or increase their savings or invest their money. What you have effectively done in steps #1–4 is create a plan to reach your goal retirement on your terms. It's in your reach.

Put there is a piece of the puzzle missing. The formula to wealth is to grow and *invest* your margin. So far, we have grown the margin necessary for financial freedom. Now we need to invest it. By investing our money, we take advantage of compound interest. And compound interest is magic. In fact, Einstein has been quoted as saying it is the most powerful force in the universe. It never rests. It can be working against you or for you. It works against you in the form of interest on debt. It works for you in the form of yield or return on investments; yield not only on your original investment amount or principal, but also on your investment earnings as they grow.

The sooner you can have compound interest stop working against you by paying off debts, as we discussed in this chapter, and get it working for you by investing wisely, the sooner you will reach financial freedom! But investing can seem very risky and complex. Is there a way to invest that minimizes risk while maximizes returns over the long term?

Chapter 10
Investing Your Money the Right Way

There are a lot of different ways to invest your money. You can invest in real estate, in venture capital enterprises, in horse races, in savings accounts…or in the stock market. Before my financial education, investing in the stock market basically seemed like investing in a horse race (gambling). It felt random, risky, and very complicated.

Admittedly, my opinion of stock market investing was largely formed based on opinions of others who had invested inappropriately and got burned as well as by the incredible amount of conflicting and loud information out there on the topic. It seemed every "financial guru" was screaming that they were right about this stock or that. And some other guru was yelling the opposite thing and that the other expert was wrong. It was the equivalent of my fantasy football league arguing over who the best running back is in a given year…uninformed and wrong 80% of the time. (We'll get back to that 80% later…)

All of the cacophony and confusion led me to the conclusion that stock market investing was just too risky and complicated. However, this is not the case. Investing wisely in the stock market is relatively simple. In fact, by learning some basic concepts, I went from clueless to managing my own investments in a month. You can too.

However, before we get started, it is important that we review a few terms and definitions that will come up. In simplified terms:

A **stock** is a part ownership in a company. You buy one share (or stock) and you become an owner. Each share has a price tag when you buy it that changes based on various and, at times, arbitrary factors as they are traded in the stock market. If the price goes up, good for you, you just made money. If it goes down…not so lucky. Stocks are generally considered higher risk investments with a greater potential return…but also a greater potential loss.

A **bond** is basically an IOU from the government, a corporation, or other entity. You give them money and they promise you to give that amount of money back with a fixed interest rate at a later date (called the maturity of the bond, like 5 years, 7

© The Author(s), under exclusive license to Springer Nature
Switzerland AG 2023
J. D. Frey, *Money Matters in Medicine*,
https://doi.org/10.1007/978-3-031-27300-1_10

years, etc.). Bonds are generally considered safer, more conservative investments compared to stocks with a lower expected return but also lower potential loss.

A **mutual fund** is a collection of stocks that a financial advisor or "expert" puts together that she or he thinks will perform very well i.e. the value will overall trend upward.

An **index fund** is a collection of stocks strategically picked to mirror some index marker of the overall stock market. For instance, the S&P 500 is an index with a collection of stocks thought to give a good sense of the overall stock market (Is the overall stock market going up or down?). An index fund will mirror the movement of the index that it is based on.

With these definitions in mind, there are many ways that you can invest in the stock market. You can invest in individual stocks of individual companies. You can invest by actively picking a collection of stocks in a mutual fund. Or you can try to mirror the overall stock market with an index fund.

As I alluded to above, we want to develop a strategy to invest in the stock market that maximizes potential return while minimizing potential risk and loss. So, which way best accomplishes this?

Picking individual stocks of individual companies does not meet this guiding criterion. As an example, imagine that you are investing 30 years ago. If you invested in Apple stock, you would have made a ton of money today and be very happy! However, if you invested in Enron stock, you would have lost everything. Through the lens of retrospect, it is easy to point out why Enron was a bad stock and Apple was a good one. However, 30 years ago, you could find just as many financial "experts" touting Enron as a "sure-thing" as there were saying the same thing about Apple. Those who bet right did well. Those who didn't lost it all. That is gambling and speculating, not investing. And we are looking to invest.

If investing in individual stocks falls short, then perhaps actively picking many individual stocks and investing in them as a mutual fund is the answer. However, all that a mutual fund does is place multiple bets on individual stock instead of just one. Investing in multiple companies, especially if their industries don't necessarily correlate, will provide diversification, and offer some protection to your portfolio of investments. But the flaws inherent in speculating in individual stocks prevails.

The only remaining option is investing in index funds. However, this option is completely passive. By design, index funds contain a broadly diversified collection of stocks to represent the entire stock market. We do not pick the best ones after careful analysis of various factors when we invest in index funds. We don't even need a financial advisor to offer their opinion to invest in index funds. All we do is simply buy and index fund and do nothing. This can't be the best option, can it?

Almost shockingly, index fund investing is the answer! Over the long term (and remember, we are only investing money for the long term), the overall stock market has always steadily increased. If you placed your money in the overall stock market at any time in history and just left it there for 20 years, you would have made a very successful investment. To visualize this, open the stock application on your phone and select the overall stock market. Select a time window of 1 day and you will see it go up and down with no particular trend, rhyme, or reason. Now start slowing zooming out...to a 1-week time window...now 1 month...now 1 year. At this point, you still see a seemingly impossible to interpret EKG reading. So, keep zooming out...to 5-years...10 years...20 years...now you can see that the overall trend of the stock market is steadily upward to the tune of roughly 7% annually over the history of the stock market.

As this exercise visually demonstrates, betting on the whole stock market is a much safer bet. Over the long term, the overall stock market has always gone up. But why? Well, when you buy the whole U.S. stock market, you are saying that you believe in the overall ingenuity and innovation of humankind and the U.S. economy. Same goes when you invest in the whole international stock market.

And this is largely what you are doing by investing in broadly diversified index funds. Most investment brokerages will have an index fund of every stock in the entire U.S. stock market. Buy that index fund and you own the next Enron, but you also own the next Apple. And everything in between. You will be investing in the innovation and entrepreneurial spirit of humankind.

This is all well and good. However, the evidence remains largely theoretical at this point. The clincher however is that multiple peer-reviewed studies have demonstrated that passive investing (with index funds) beats active investing (with individual stocks or actively managed mutual funds) 80% of the time each year! Further, the 20% who beat the passive investors are no more likely to beat them the following year. And we are not talking about hobbyists day trading in their basements with these figures. We are talking about Wall Street.

Combine this with the fact that active investing strategies incur significantly more fees and taxes that eat into your returns, and passive investing in the stock market with broadly diversified, low-cost index funds becomes simple favorite. This strategy meets our criteria of maximizing returns while minimizing risk right on the nose.

What's even better is that you can invest in more than just stocks using index funds. There are total bond market index funds that you can invest in. There are even index fund-type investments in real estate called Real Estate Investment Trusts (REITs) to invest in.

Now that we know investing via index funds is the way to go, the question becomes how should we divvy our index funds up. We need to determine our asset allocation, the proportion of stocks, bonds, and possibly real estate that we invest in via index funds.

There are a lot of thoughts on this topic and not many ways that you can go wrong. A good rule of thumb is that your age rounded down to the nearest 10 is the percentage of bonds that you should have. You can then alter this up or down based on if you would like to be more or less conservative, respectively. The point is that as you get older, your goal becomes less and less to grow your nest egg and more and more to conserve it. A higher bond percentage or allocation accomplishes this.

For this example, let's say that I want an asset allocation of 80% U.S. stocks and 20% bonds. Of course, you could add some international stocks as well. And there are many other subcategories available to bring into the fold. But no need to get overly complex. A simple "two or three fund" portfolio with the overall U.S. and international stock markets and U.S. bond market is completely sufficient. You can also split you bond allocation to include some inflation-protected bonds.

Now is the easy part. Take the total money that you are going to invest and multiply it by each percentage. That is equal to the amount that you will put into each index fund. After you do that, you don't need to do anything for a year. Because you are prudent and only invested money that you will not need for 15–20 years. If the market goes up, down, or sideways tomorrow or next month or next year, you don't care. You don't care what the talking heads on TV or in the newspaper say. Over the long term, you know that your investments will rise because you are smart and bet on the ingenuity of humankind rather than try to stock pick or time the market, which no one in history has been able to do reliably. In fact, by managing your portfolio this way (passively), statistics show that you have a portfolio that is *better* than 80% of people in any given year who try to actively "beat the market."

When investing in anything, the goal is to buy low and sell high. Then you earn the difference between the buying price and the selling price. But how can you do this in the market without timing it or guessing the future, which we know we cannot reliably do? Again, the answer is simple.

After you buy your funds in your asset allocation, do nothing. Then once or twice a year, rebalance your portfolio back to your set asset allocation. Here's an example of how to do this. Some years, stocks will do better than bonds. At the end of the year using our example, you may have 90% stocks and 10% bonds (because stocks performed better than bonds). To rebalance, you would sell enough stocks (you are selling high) and buy enough bonds (you are buying low) to get your allocation back at 80% stocks and 20% bonds. Do this and you are guaranteed to always sell high and buy low. And studies demonstrate that rebalancing your asset allocation over the long term offers a return benefit.

Alternatively, you can divvy up whatever new funds you will be investing in the correct proportion to rebalance your asset allocation back to its predetermined percentages. This way, you can just buy low and don't need to sell (and risk any tax implications). Now sit back another year and do the same thing.

After reviewing this investing strategy, I often am asked if physicians need to have a financial advisor. My answer is simple. You do not need a financial advisor to manage your money as a physician. I went from financially clueless to managing my own finances within a few months. And there's nothing particularly special about me. If I can do it, so can you. It's largely about mindset, you have learned so many more difficult things than the basics of investing your money. You can do it!

With that said though, I am not opposed to someone paying a fair price for good advice from a financial advisor. But you do have to be able to generally tell good advice from bad advice as well as what a fair price is for this to work. So, you need to be educated regardless. And frankly, by the time you are educated enough to tell this difference, you are also educated enough to manage your own finances.

Regardless, let's review some things to know about financial advisors in case you decide to use one. You should interview the advisor and don't take it easy on him or her. This person is managing your money, the money that you earned after spending countless hours studying, not sleeping, and helping patients. Don't throw it away.

You will want to ask how the advisor makes their money. If they tell you that you don't pay them or you don't understand their answer, this means that they are paid by commissions they make from selling you bad investments. This is not a good arrangement. If they tell you they get a percentage of what you make, it's worth learning more and perhaps negotiating a bit. A usual fee is 1% of assets under management. This means that they get 1% of your total investments with them. At least with this model, your goals are aligned. If you do well, they do well. But once your portfolio gets greater in value, are they really working harder to deserve to get paid more? The best fee structure is a flat fee service where you pay a flat fee for the work that your advisor does. There are those out there who do this so look for them or contact me for a recommendation.

Ask your potential advisor what their investment strategy is. Do they think they can beat the market by actively managing your money. There is an 80% chance that they cannot do this while this strategy will cost you money in taxes and fees. As I will show you shortly, they should be proponents of or at least open to managing your money with passive low cost, broadly diversified index funds. Also make sure that you like them. If you get a bad feeling, don't go with them. It's not worth it. Ultimately the decision to use a financial advisor is personal despite not being necessary. Just make sure you understand what services they are offering and how much you are paying for them.

We have so far covered the *why*, *what*, and *how* of investing your money on the path to financial freedom. But there is still one very important aspect that we need to address, *Where* should we invest our money?

Chapter 11
Invest in the Right Places

To review, your simple formula to reach financial freedom as a physician is to save at least 20% of your income, invest in broadly diversified low-cost index funds along with bonds and possibly real estate according to your chosen asset allocation and then re-balance yearly.

But there remains the question of *where* to put your investments. The *where* consists of the various types of investment accounts available that you can utilize to invest.

The best way to think about these investment accounts is that they are like buckets that you put your money into. Within each bucket, you can choose the type of investment that you would like to invest in…like broadly diversified low-cost index funds. Moreover, each investment account, or bucket, has special features, advantages, and disadvantages.

In this chapter, I'll review some of the more common investment accounts available to most people, especially physicians, as well as their pros and cons. In general, your goal will be to prioritize these buckets based on their advantages. Then you will fill the first bucket (investment account) with money until it reaches the maximum amount. After this, your savings and investments above this amount will spill into the next bucket/investment account on your priority list. I like to think about this as a waterfall with each bucket spilling into the next.

It is important to recognize however that doctors saving at least 20% of their income will need many, if not all, buckets in order to grow their margin sufficiently to reach financial freedom. That is why understanding *where* you can invest your margin is so important.

The first account we'll review is a **taxable investment account**. This is the account that most people think of when they image investing money in the stock market. This account does not carry any special considerations from the government or IRS. And anyone can open one of these accounts by signing up for one online with any brokerage like Vanguard or Fidelity for instance.

© The Author(s), under exclusive license to Springer Nature Switzerland AG 2023
J. D. Frey, *Money Matters in Medicine*,
https://doi.org/10.1007/978-3-031-27300-1_11

In general, the money that you put into this account has already been taxed via income taxes (post-tax money) and any money made in the account is taxed when you take it out via capital gains taxes. These taxes can be either lower rate long term capital gains taxes or higher rate short term capital gains taxes depending if you keep the money in the account for more or less than 1 year.

However, you can remove the money from the account at any time without a penalty. Other accounts, as you will see, have age limits for withdrawal. Take money out before a certain age limit and you will be penalized. This is not the case with taxable accounts. Additionally, there is no limit to the amount of money that you can invest in a taxable account. All tax-advantaged accounts as discussed below will have a annual limit for contributions.

In general, you will want to contribute the maximum to your tax advantaged accounts (below) before contributing to your taxable account. This minimizes your tax burden—a big goal for high income earners like physicians.

A **401(k) investment account** is probably the most common retirement investment account offered by employers. Additionally, self-employed individuals can open a **solo 401(k)**.

In a 401(k), the money you put in each year (limited to $20,500 in 2022) is not yet taxed (pre-tax money). It then grows in the account and is taxed when you withdraw the money in the future. This is advantageous because your effective tax rate during your peak earning years is likely to higher than it will be in retirement when you will take the money out.

Often, employers will also contribute to your 401(k) as well. Commonly, a "match" is offered in which the employer will contribute a certain amount if you contribute to the 401k to a certain level. The maximum combined employer-employee contribution in 2022 is $58,000. If you are self-employed with a solo 401(k), don't worry. You can contribute as both the employer and employee.

The price for this tax advantage is that the money cannot be withdrawn prior to age 59½. Take the money out before that age and you will pay a 10% penalty in addition to the typical taxes. Another disadvantage is that the types of investments that are available in a 401(k) (or 403(b) and 457 below) are limited to those offered by the brokerage that your employer hired to sponsor the plan. Though rare, it is therefore possible that your 401(k) would not offer low cost, diversified index funds to invest in. In these cases, you will need to weigh the benefits of the tax advantages in the 401(k) versus the benefits of investing with lower fees using index funds without tax advantages in a taxable account.

By broad strokes, a **403(b) account** is very similar to a 401(k) with the exception that it is available to employees of public schools and certain tax-exempt organizations like public hospitals. My current retirement plan with my employer is via a 403(b).

A **457 investment account** is another tax advantaged retirement account. It comes in two flavors: **governmental 457** and **non-governmental 457**.

Governmental 457 accounts are more common and cater to local and state public workers rather than for-profit employers like 401(k)s. Non-governmental 457s are available to certain tax-exempt non-governmental institutions. They are similar but, in general, governmental 457s are a bit better.

Like 401(k)s, 457s allow pre-tax contributions that grow within the account and are taxed upon withdrawal. The 2020 contribution limit is $20,500. While employer contributions are possible, the total limit stays $20,500. This means that if your employer will contribute $10,000, you can only contribute $10,500.

The disadvantage again is that you can only withdraw from this account without a 10% penalty at age 70½ or for other qualified emergencies. The other downside is that for 457s, the money you contribute technically becomes your employer's money until you withdraw it again. This means that if your employer folds, your 457 contributions and returns are lost. That is why governmental 457s are considered superior. The government is much less likely to default compared to a private company.

Next, a **Traditional IRA** or **Individual Retirement Account** is an investment account available to any individual generating income of any kind. Basically, if you are working, you are entitled to open an IRA. And you can do so with any brokerage just by going online.

You can contribute up to $6000 yearly (as of 2022) to a Traditional IRA. Money put into this account is not taxed. Again, the money grows and then is taxed upon withdrawal (when your effective tax rate is likely lower). Money can be withdrawn without a 10% penalty beginning at age 70½.

The main issue with a Traditional IRA is that the initial tax deduction upon contributing money is phased out for individuals making more than $75,000 or married couples making more than $125,000 in 2022. Physicians will be above this income limit and therefore, their contributions will be taxed twice—once at contribution and once at withdrawal. Thus, this type of investment account would offer no advantage compared to a regular taxable account. In fact, the IRA would be worse because there is an age minimum for penalty-free withdrawal as well as a yearly contribution limit.

Before I get into the way around this IRA issue, I'll introduce the **Roth IRA**. The Roth IRA is named after Senator William Roth who introduced the concept. With a Roth IRA, your money is taxed at the time of contribution. The money then grows tax-free and is NOT taxed upon withdrawal. The contribution limit in 2022 is $6000 and the general rule for age of withdrawal without penalty is 59½.

However, once again, there is an income limit to be allowed to contribute to a Roth IRA and receive these tax advantages. The income limit in 2022 is $139,000 for individuals and $206,000 for married couples. Most attending physicians will again be above these limits. However, this is a great investment account for resident physicians who will be below the income limit. Residents can thus contribute directly to a Roth IRA when they are in the lowest tax bracket that they will ever be in. Then their contributions can grow and be withdrawn tax free in the future!

With that being said, there is however a way for high income earners to contribute to a Roth IRA. It is colloquially called a **Backdoor Roth IRA**. To illustrate, let's say your income as a married couple is above $206,000. You already maxed out your 401(k) and 457(b) options. You want to maximize your tax advantaged investing before contributing into a taxable investment account. What you can do is contribute $6000 to a Traditional IRA. Because you are above the income limit, your contributions will then be taxed. If you leave it in the Traditional IRA, your money will be taxed again upon withdrawal. But, the government will now allow you to roll your (now after-tax) Traditional IRA contributions into a Roth IRA once a year. Once this rollover is done, the money will grow tax free and not be taxed upon withdrawal. You are contributing to a Roth IRA legally through the backdoor…hence the nickname.

Next, I will briefly mention **529** and **HSA (Health Savings Account) accounts**. A **529 account** is an education savings account. You contribute money tax free, invest it tax free, and withdraw it tax free so long as it goes towards your designated child's qualified educational expenses. Qualified expanses can be found on the IRS website. Any money withdrawn for non-qualified expenses get hit with an extra 10% penalty in addition to usual taxes. But don't worry, if you have money left over from one dependent's 529 account, you can always transfer it to another dependent or relative with education expenses.

An **HSA** meanwhile is an account available only to members of high-deductible insurance plans where you contribute tax free money to be used towards health care expenses. While in the account, it grows tax free and is withdrawn tax free, so long as it goes towards health care expenses. Thus, when used appropriately, the HSA is triple tax-free.

The extra nice trick with an HSA is that you don't need to withdraw money to pay for health care expenses right when they are due. You can save the receipt for a health expense in the current year and withdraw the money from your HSA years later tax free using your saved receipt after it has had years to benefit from compound interest growth.

There are a variety of other more advanced tax-advantaged investment accounts, especially for self-employed physicians and individuals. These include **cash balance plans**, **SEP-IRAs**, **profit sharing plans**, and beyond. If you are self-employed and interested in learning more about these tax-advantages accounts, I recommend seeking out and consulting with an experienced tax advisor.

I will also briefly mention **pensions**. While not as common as they were in the past, pensions are a type of defined-benefit plan compared to 401(k) accounts and the rest discussed above, which are defined-contribution plans. Pensions work as you contribute a certain, fixed annual amount to the pension. Your employer then invests the collective contributions as they see fit with a. promise to pay you a fixed amount of income during your retirement. The risk here is that your employer may not invest their pensions wisely resulting in lost money and evaporating pension payments for retirees. If deciding between a pension and a defined-contribution retirement plan, carefully consider all advantages and disadvantages of both within the context of your financial goals and seek professional assistance as necessary.

As I mentioned at the start of this chapter, our goal is to organize these accounts or buckets into a waterfall based on their advantages given our unique financial situations. Once organized into the waterfall, we can just contribute money into the first bucket until it overflows into the second bucket and so on (Fig. 11.1).

Fig. 11.1 Example investment waterfall

While everyone's financial situation and therefore investment account waterfall will be personal, I will provide a very reasonable example here:

1. **401(k) or 403(b)**
2. **457(b)**
3. **Backdoor Roth IRA (if you are above income limits for direct IRA contribution)**
4. If you are under the income limits for direct IRA contribution, favor a **Traditional IRA** if your tax rate is higher now than later or a **Roth IRA** if your tax rate will be higher later than it is now.
5. **529 (if you have dependents with current or expected education expenses)**
6. **HSA (if your insurance plan qualifies as high deductible)**
7. **Taxable Account**

You now understand not only the rules of the game, but the strategies that will lead you to win the game of wealth building and financial freedom. That is incredibly empowering! I truly do believe that a nation and world of financially free doctors can change healthcare for the better in ways that we cannot currently imagine. And you are helping do that!

I'd like to go back to our formula for wealth. Grow and invest the margin between what you make and what you spend. Now that we have the basics down, how can we refine our strategies even further to maximize our wealth? One of the most powerful of these strategies may come as a surprise…spending money.

Chapter 12
Spending Is the Key to Your Wealth

It seems counterintuitive that spending money is the key to building wealth. But that is because when we think of spending money, we are really thinking about spending money *unintentionally*. Because this is the way we see others spend money and has become the default way that we spend our money as well. The real key therefore becomes learning to spend money *intentionally*. Then, we become in full control of our wealth building equation.

Intentional spending also plays a huge role in our happiness and fulfillment. It turns the focus on your money spent back on yourself, instead of where it usually is, which is on the goods or services that you spent the money on. Let me explain further. Intentional spending is the concept that one is intentional with the money that she or he spends. Meaning that any purchase is well thought out and carries an intended purpose.

To round out this definition, we do need to define the opposite of intentional spending—unintentional spending. Unintentional spending is what most of us do most of the time. It's a bit of a reflex. We spend our money without really focusing and even thinking about if what we spend it on is making us happy. And research has shown that humans are incredibly bad at predicting what will make us happy—especially with our purchases.

As a quick example, can you think of a time where you bought something that you thought would bring a lot of entertainment, joy, fulfillment, use? How long did the excitement of that purchase last? How long did its usefulness last? And how long did it fulfill you? If you are like me (and most of humanity), the purchase caused a brief hit of dopamine after which the excitement faded as did the utility of the purchase. It's a frustrating experience that many of us live over repeatedly.

The solution to this vicious cycle is intentional spending. And the key with intentional spending is that the absolute dollar value of the purchase is completely irrelevant in your decision-making. You should go through the same mental calculus whether a purchase is $1 or $10,000. And the more that you can practice this, the more it will become second nature and feel like an automated thought process.

J. D. Frey, *Money Matters in Medicine*,
https://doi.org/10.1007/978-3-031-27300-1_12

I still actively practice the mental exercise of intentional spending and will still catch myself making unintentional purchases. And that is fine. The point is to improve. There is no perfection, like everything else.

Before getting into the actual formula, let's examine why are doctors so bad at intentional spending to begin with. To be fair, all people are bad at intentional spending. We spend un-intentionally. We buy something, get a short dopamine hit, then it wears off and we forget about that good or service. But doctors are particularly bad at intentional spending. Why?

Because we have experienced years of delayed gratification. We make little money and go deep into debt during our prime years during our training. During this time, we watch non-doctor friends spend money on things like cars, homes, and toys (although they are likely doing so unintentionally as well). In the meantime, our time is severely constrained by training. By the time we finish training, we are primed to spend to try and make up for lost time. This begets rampant unintentional spending. It's hard to blame anyone in this position.

At this point, I will clarify that I am by no means saying not to spend money. However, I am saying that you need to spend money *intentionally*. Otherwise, you will get caught in a very bad place financially. You will become the high income, low net worth doctors who are living paycheck to paycheck and working beyond when they want to. This is the opposite of financial freedom. And we don't want that.

So, how can we all practice intentional spending? Thankfully, there is a simple formula that we can use to practice intentional spending. With every purchase that you make, whether the absolute dollar value of the purchase is $1 or $1 million, answer the following questions:

- Can I make this purchase and still reach my financial goals within my desired time frame?
- Is the joy derived from the purchase greater than or equal to the dollar value of the purchase?

If the answer to both questions is yes, then you should make the purchase. If the answer to either question is no, then you should walk away from the purchase. This simple thought experiment changes our whole mindset around the purchases that we make. It increases the satisfaction we receive from our purchases and hard-earned money. Because remember, money is only valuable as a tool to bring joy to ourselves, our loved ones, and the world at large. We undercut this whole ideal when we spend unintentionally. But with intentional spending, we bring everything back into harmony.

Breaking it down further, let's imagine you are considering a purchase. Forget what it is and forget how much but actually costs. If you can make that purchase while still following your financial plan (which is leading you to your financial goals), that's a great thing. If you consider the purchase thoughtfully and deliberately to determine that the joy from that purchase is greater than it's purchase price, even better. In this case, why would you *not* make that purchase?! It doesn't make sense.

On the flip side, if you cannot stick to your financial plan while also making that purchase, then you cannot afford that purchase. And, if you consider the purchase thoughtfully and deliberately and determine that the joy from that purchase is *not* greater than its purchase price, well, that seals it. In the above case, why would you *make* that purchase?! It doesn't make sense.

The logic is quite simple. But this a thought process we almost always glaze over or ignore completely. Why is that?

The most obvious reason that most of us reflexively avoid the intentional spending thought model is that most people don't have a budget or written financial plan. Therefore, they don't know if their spending is aligned with their financial goals or overall joy. Without an end in sight, we can't plot the course and so we ignore or avoid it.

You have already started to create the solution to this problem just by reading this book. You know the formula to build wealth and reach financial freedom. You have the tools to create your own budget and spending plan. You now know the formula for intentional spending to bring your spending plan into harmony with your goals and your joys. And in Chap. 15, we will tie everything together and work to develop our own personal financial plan.

The other big reason that we all too often forgo thinking about intentional spending is that, like I said earlier, humans are just incredibly bad at determining the joy that they will receive from purchases. Of course, this will always be an intangible estimation. But we are bad at making this estimation. The dopaminergic pathways of our brains are very powerful and impede our ability to accurately assess the long-term satisfaction of our actions. That is why humans are all too likely to favor decisions with short term gains but carrying long-term negative consequences.

In any regard, there is a solution to this issue. And, not surprisingly, it is quite simple. Wait. When you want to make a purchase, just wait. Wait at least 2 weeks. If you still want it and believe it will bring you joy greater than the price tag, go for it. If you don't still want it, chances are that you never really did. Instead, you were likely just looking for that dopamine hit. Study after study has shown that the longer we wait before a purchase, the more we enjoy it. And I can confirm this from personal experience.

I want to drive home the importance of intentional spending with two personal examples. First, at the risk of losing you all, I am going to make an admission. I am not a car person. I just don't care much about cars. Really, I just want something functional and reliable to take me from point A to point B. But, when I was about to become an attending physician, I ear marked about $1000/month to lease a luxury car.

As I thought about it more, this didn't make any sense. While I could fit it into my financial plan, the joy that the lease would bring me was decidedly less than the cost. So, I made a change. I cancelled the lease and bought a used Toyota for $4000. This car meets my goals and brings me joy greater than its price tag. I also now have an additional $1000/month that I can use to further grow and invest my margin or to spend intentionally on goods or services that will bring me a commensurate joy.

But let me make one thing very clear, if that car did bring me more joy than the price and worked within my financial plan, I would have spent the money. I'm not saying to be overly frugal or not spend money at all. I am just saying to spend it intentionally. To prove this point, let's move on to the next example.

Whenever I first introduce this concept of intentional spending, people think that I am a spending prude, advocating to save everything and buy nothing. But that's not the case. I just want you to spend intentionally. In fact, when I graduated, I bought what can only be deemed a "doctor house." This is not the typical recommendation from a financial standpoint. And it is not what I recommend to graduating trainees. (The most generalizable advice would be to rent for a few years while you ensure that you like your new job and its location before buying a house when you become an attending physician.)

However, we found a house that met our criteria in terms of what we were looking for, fit in our financial plan, and continues to bring us greater joy that the price tag. That price tag is not small, but the purchase checked both boxes of the intentional spending thought experiment, so we bought it.

The moral of the story with intentional spending is that spending money is not bad. Money is simply a tool. A tool that I believe should be used for the betterment of yourself, your loved ones, and your world community. With that definition, not spending money would be bad. But at the same time, to spend that money unintentionally in a way that does not accomplish those goals would be wasteful. So, the key is to spend money intentionally—for your happiness and for your wealth.

Now that we have further refined the "what you spend" portion, we need to address the "what you make" side of the wealth building equation. And while what you make is not as in your control as what you spend, we can certainly optimize it with very concrete and actionable strategies.

Chapter 13
Increasing your Clinical and Non-clinical Income

Now it's time to discuss specific and actionable strategies to maximize your income as a physician. Doing so optimizes the "what you make" side of the wealth building margin equation. As a physician, there are three main areas in which we can optimize our compensation:

1. Contract negotiation
2. Clinical income
3. Non-clinical income

Contract Negotiation

For those physicians in your last year of training, you will soon be negotiating your first contract. This is an exciting thing, but it's also scary since it will have such a massive impact on your financial future, and we have very little preparation with regards to contract negotiation. Even if you already have an attending job, I'll bet there are aspects of your contract that you want to improve during your next negotiation.

I graduated in July 2020 which means that I recently found my job and then negotiated and signed a contract successfully. I'm not saying my contract is perfect. But it fits me very well. And that's what you want, a contract that fits your goals, circumstances, and well-being.

Contract negotiation is the time when you set the foundation for what you will make and how you will make it. There is usually some wiggle room within the contract to make more or less over time. However, you largely set the scale of your physician income as soon as you sign on the dotted line.

Let's now review all of the things that you will need to know to successfully negotiate a contract!

© The Author(s), under exclusive license to Springer Nature
Switzerland AG 2023
J. D. Frey, *Money Matters in Medicine*,
https://doi.org/10.1007/978-3-031-27300-1_13

1. **Make your negotiation personal**

   It's about your situation and not anyone else's. Everyone will prioritize different things in their contracts. Your contract is an individual competition. You are not trying to get the best contract compared to your peers or anything like that. You want the best contract for you. Focus internally and ask how you could alter things to be the best for you.

2. **Know your value**

   This may be the best single piece of advice that I received regarding contract negotiation. I heard it from a number of my mentors. It sounds so obvious that it almost doesn't seem helpful at first. But really, this is going to be the crux of your negotiation. You can be sure that the administrators negotiating the contract with you know exactly how much value the average physician in your position brings. You had better know that as well…and then know why you are *way more* valuable than the average physician in your field.

   But how do you find out your value in terms of compensation?

   It can be a little intimidating to go about finding out this numeric value. We never really talk about money with our colleagues or mentors. We feel embarrassed. But we shouldn't.

   Here is how you find your value. I did all of these things:

   • Ask your mentors how much they make and how their contract is structured
   • Ask recent graduates in your field how much they make and how things went negotiating their contract
   • Find out how many relative value units (RVUs) the average physician in your field does annually. Then find the average $/RVU value in your field (It's $65/ RVU for plastic surgeons). Multiple these two numbers and you have a good sense of what your annual salary should be.
   • Make a list of the unique skills that you have that make you more valuable than an average physician in your field. For me, it was my training, research abilities, and even my ability to do robotic surgeries.

   Once you know your value, you have a reference to negotiate with. You know what fair compensation is. Once you are in that range in negotiating your contract, you can get further into the details.

3. **Pick how you would like to make your money: base versus incentives**

   I'll give an example from negotiating my contract. Like most physicians, I am highly motivated by incentives. I will chase the carrot forever. But what I realized is that this endless pursuit ultimately frustrated me and contributed to my burn out. Therefore, I sought a contract with minimally incentive-based pay. I negotiated a contract with a base salary that represented 96% of my total salary. The remaining 4% was performance-based.

   For a surgeon, this is not a typical arrangement. Most contracts are performance-based using the amount of relative value units (RVUs) generated by the surgeon. This leads to RVU chasing and, for me, takes the focus off the patient and the work that I have a passion for.

   So, I was very happy to take a base salary that paid me a very good amount of money that I could grow through smart investing and live very comfortably. This allows me to focus on the portions of my job that I love the most, patient care and operating, without worrying about patient insurance type, optimizing reimbursement, or making sure I reach and exceed a certain RVU goal, lest I see my salary decrease if I don't meet it.

Now I understand that many people may desire a strong incentive component in their salary. This is fine as long as it aligns with what will make you the most fulfilled, decrease risk of burnout, and allow you to pursue financial well-being.

4. **Create the ability to safely move on if things don't work out**

Another aspect of contract negotiation that I feel is particularly important is optimizing your potential exit. You never want to go into a job thinking that it will not work out. But the reality is that these arrangements often do not go as intended. In the case that you find yourself unhappy with things, you want to make sure that you can make changes that improve your life without restriction. The most important terms in this regard are your contract length and the existence or nature of your non-compete clause.

I negotiated a relatively short contract (3 years). I feel that this amount of time allows for both parties to make a good faith effort at making the relationship work, even if there are bumps in the road. After 3 years, I will be free to re-negotiate according to the value that I bring to my employer at that point or to move on. I plan to be there for a long time but it's nice to know that you are not trapped. That's another feeling that can and will lead to burnout.

The non-compete clause is a big factor in your ability to move on. For those unfamiliar, a non-compete clause essentially says in varying terms that if you leave this job you cannot work within X miles of the job site for a certain length of times, usually 1–3 years. If you are like me and moved to your hometown to raise your family, you would not want a contract that tells you to work at least 50 miles away if the relationship does not pan out.

If you are moving somewhere with a temporary plan or would not stay in that city without being at that job, then a non-compete may not be as big of a deal to you. But who knows, maybe in time you find that you love this geographic area and want to stay even after leaving your current job situation.

The least restrictive non-compete clause is obviously to your greatest advantage. Many will tell you that it is a standard part of the contract, however everything is negotiable. Maybe you even agree to take less money to reduce or eliminate the constraints of the non-compete clause.

I found my particular opportunity so appealing because the group that I was joining had negotiated for no non-compete clauses in their contracts. I used their precedent to remove the clause from my contract.

5. **Learn your benefits, they are part of your salary too!**

Another overlooked aspect of contract negotiation is making sure that you have a comprehensive understanding of the benefits offered by your employer.

Your benefits package makes the difference in tens of thousands of dollars but most people don't even learn about them until after signing the contract. Ask to speak with a benefits representative during your interview or on the phone.

Find out what tax protected retirement accounts are offered and specifically if the employer offers a match. Let's say the employer will contribute up to $22,800 to a retirement account like mine. That's $22,800 additional money that will grow tax free via compound interest that is basically a part of your contract. As an aside, make certain that *you* contribute enough to your retirement account to trigger the employer match. Failing to do so is leaving money at the negotiating table.

Also find out if your employer offers a Health Savings Account (HSA). I won't go into detail about HSAs here, but in brief, it is one of the very few triple tax free investment vehicles and is a nice advantage if they have one (my employer does not).

Learn if your employer offers group malpractice, disability, or life insurance and how much it covers. This will reduce or eliminate the need to buy expensive individual policies on your own dime. The malpractice insurance that my group offers is so strong that I did not need an individual policy. The life insurance, however, was minimal and no group disability is offered so I did purchase these on my own.

6. **The deal is in the details**

   If you are joining a private practice or partnership, make sure that the details of your partnership track are completely spelled out to the last detail in your contract. Find out how long it will take to become partner. What is the buy-in? How do the partners split profits? Do they split them evenly or based on seniority? You don't want to go into a situation with the implication that you will be made partner in 2 years to find out that it actually will take 7 years and require a significant buy-in. Again, this can lead to mistrust, job, and financial dissatisfaction, and burn out. This was not an issue with the hospital-based job that I took but was something that I made sure was very clear with other potential opportunities.

7. **If it's not in the contract, it doesn't count!**

   This ties into another really important point. Anything not written and signed in your contract does not count. No handshake agreements, no verbal promises, nothing. If something is important to you, make sure it is written clear in the contract. If they balk at doing this, they either promised you something that they can't guarantee or are not operating in good faith.

8. **Don't be shy, just ask!**

   The great thing about contracts is that really nothing is off limits in negotiation. As long as your are reasonable and respectful, the worst that the other side can say is "no". So just ask. I was told "no" for a couple of the "asks" in my contract. But rather than get upset, I just used those "no's" to help get a "yes" to two in other parts of my contract.

9. **Crowdsource your negotiations**

   Lastly, have a ton of people read your contract and get their advice and opinions. You don't need to listen to everything or follow each piece of advice, but the more eyes on it the better. You can even send me your contract, I'd be happy to look it over. Don't be bashful to share the specifics of your contract and encourage others to talk openly about their contract. This will only help all of us to negotiate the best situations.

   And hire a lawyer to review the contract. By the end of my negotiations, I had so many eyeballs, notably my own, review the contract so many times that the lawyer didn't have a ton to add. But it still made me feel more reassured and was the final piece of the puzzle before signing.

And then, once you sign your contract, celebrate! Not only did you just sign a contract to live your dream and be a physician, helping others. But you just signed your dream contract because you took the time to really think it through and make it the best arrangement for both sides!

Remember, your contract negotiation is your opportunity to set the stage for your financial and personal success. Don't miss the opportunity to ask for what you want. You worked extremely hard to get to this point and offer very specialized skills that help people. I absolutely encourage you to know your value (and your values) and use your contract negotiation period to create the best opportunity *for you* out in the open market!

Utilizing Your Sign-on Bonus

I also want to make special mention of the sign-on bonus that the majority of physicians will and should receive with their contract. This is because I can usually determine how a physician will do financially by knowing how they spend their sign-on bonus as well as their first paycheck.

While not a part of every contract, a lump sum sign on bonus is typical of the majority of physician contracts. If you receive an offer letter or contract without such a bonus, I highly recommend negotiating for one.

It is important to remember that this bonus is income. And therefore it is subject to income taxes. So, some amount will generally be withheld by your (future) employer. If not, you should self withhold some of the bonus. Or else you will be in for a surprise come tax time.

And lastly, the sign on bonus usually comes with a stipulation. And that stipulation stipulates (forgive me) that you only keep the bonus if you work with the employer for a certain amount of time. Usually that term is 1 year. If you leave early, you need to pay it back.

With this understood, let's move on to the best uses for these bonuses and break this up into two realities…

In an Ideal World

Remember, the formula to build wealth and reach financial freedom is to create and grow your margin. And your margin is the difference between what you make and what you spend. While your budget and philosophy of intentional spending help you create the margin, your written financial plan will guide you in growing your margin. And your written financial plan will have a prioritized list of financial goals. Like this list in my financial plan (we will work on creating your own personal financial plan in Chap. 15!):

1. Pay down high interest loans/debt (>8%) Done! (as of 10/2020)
2. Establish emergency fund (3–6 month's expenses) Done! (as of 12/2020)
3. Maximize Voluntary Defined Contribution (VDC) retirement account

4. Pay down medium interest loans (6–8%)
5. Invest in vetted real estate (cash flowing rentals w/ cash-on-cash ratio > 10%)
6. Contribute to 529 college savings account
7. Maximize 457(b) retirement account
8. Pay extra to mortgage
9. Pay down low interest loans (<3%)
10. Contribute to back door/spousal Roth IRA (every January if contributing—2 steps)
11. Contribute to retirement taxable account
12. Donate to charity with equity dividends

Once you have a personalized financial priority list like this, the decision of what to do with any monetary windfall like a sign on bonus becomes easy. You just put the money towards your top priority. Until that priority is fulfilled. Then move on to the next priority. And so on until the bonus runs out. These priorities will be different for everyone. This underscores the importance of actually creating your very own written financial plan.

However, some common priorities for most physicians will be:

• Pay off credit card debt or other high interest debt
• Create an emergency fund
• Pay down student loans
• Invest in a Roth IRA (especially if you are still a trainee which means you are under the income limit to still contribute and are in the lowest tax bracket you will ever be in your life!
• Invest in a taxable investment account

These are all great wealth-building and financial freedom-accelerating uses for a bonus covered in detail in Chaps. 10 and 11! But we do not live in an ideal world! So let's examine our other, more accurate reality…

In Our Non-ideal World

It would be great if all of us were completely rational. And we all just used our physician sign on bonus solely to accelerate our path to financial freedom and living/working on our own terms. But that is not reality. And I think this is a good thing. So, especially when you are finishing your training and about to start your first job, some other ideas typically come to mind. Let's look at some of these more closely.

Moving Expenses

I lead off with this quickly because you should *not* have to use your sign on bonus to cover moving expenses. Your employer should cover these separately. That is what is typical. If moving expenses aren't included in your contract, negotiate them. Also remember that these are now taxable as well however.

A Down Payment on a House

Whether to buy a home right out of training or to rent a home is a very nuanced discussion. However, the more generalizable advice is to initially rent coming out of training. This gives you time to evaluate your new job and potentially new city before making a significant and not easily transferrable financial commitment.

However, in certain circumstances, buying a home out of training can make sense. For instance, that is what I did. In this case, your physician sign on bonus can be used as a down payment. Actually, you can often avoid needing a down payment using a physician home loan.

Again, you need to evaluate your own unique financial situation in light of your financial goals in determining (A) if you should buy a home out of training, (B) if you should use a physician home loan or not, and (C) if and how much a down payment to use. But this is a common and potentially acceptable alternative use for a physician sign on bonus.

Buying a Car

This may be another acceptable use for a sign on bonus. But I am much more willing to be dogmatic about if and when it is a good use here compared to above!
First, do not use it for a down payment on a car loan! If you cannot buy the car you want in cash, then you can't afford it. Simple as that. Second, if you are buying a car in cash using your bonus, make sure you are doing so intentionally as we discussed in Chap. 12!

I bought a used Toyota for $4000 after training the I still drive today. Why? Because I'm not a car person. And it didn't make sense to spend the $1000/month that I initially budgeted to lease a luxury car. Now I just use that extra $1000/month to buy other thing that bring me joy or to accelerate my path to financial freedom.

Vacation

I fully support this as a non-wealth building expense for your physician sign on bonus. The time after training but before you start your first job is the last that is truly yours before you retire. Use it and enjoy it. Spend time with your loved ones on a vacation. Obviously do so intentionally again. But this is investing in yourself and your sanity. It's ok to celebrate a bit!
As always the right answer is a somewhere in the middle. It's rare and probably not advisable that someone uses the entirety of their sign on bonus for one thing. And everyone's situation will be unique and tailored to their circumstances.

It's impossible to proscribe that there is a "right" way to use your physician sign on bonus. There is certainly a wrong way—wasting it on a thing or things that neither bring you long lasting joy nor helps you advance on the path to financial freedom. But there is no singular right way.

In fact, I really like the advice I once heard called the 10% rule. It says to take 10% of your windfall and spend it guilt free. Then save, invest, or pay of debt with the rest.

And now that we have covered contracts in depth, let's discuss strategies for optimizing your clinical income.

Optimize Your Clinical Income

Each physician will have a unique practice set up. Some may be in private practice. Others may be employed in academia or via a hospital system. Others may even primarily work locum tenens positions. We each have unique specialties lending us specific opportunities to help patients and be compensated for it. Therefore, we will focus on generalizable strategies that all physicians can utilize to optimize their clinical income. Clinically is where most of us will look to increase our compensation. It's where most of us make all or most of our money. So, it makes sense.

The first step, then, is to understand how individuals, businesses, and even physicians are compensated in our society. It's actually quite simple. And p*lease note, I am not saying that this is the right way for people to be compensated. I am merely stating that this is how it currently works.* And here it is: the less people that can offer the good or service that you offer, you more that you get paid. The converse is also true: The more people that can offer the good or service that you offer, you less that you get paid.

This does not always make intuitive or ethical or rational or utilitarian sense. But that is the way things work. It explains why LeBron James is paid way more than a cardiologist. For better or worse, many people can diagnose and treat a heart murmur. Not many people can dunk a basketball. Even less can average over 30 points a game in the NBA. It even explains why I, as a plastic surgeon, am paid much more than a primary care doctor. There are less people that do what I do in terms of reconstructive microsurgery. That certainly does not mean that my job is more important than a primary care physician. I am fortunate that my passion led me to such a position. But that is not always the case.

How can we increase our clinical compensate then? First, in your job, think about what you do. What is your role? What tasks are your responsibility? How do you create value for your employer or your business? *Now, think about how many other people do that same thing or can do the same thing as you.*

If the answer is "a lot," then you want to change this. That means that in your current position, you have no leverage or power. If you ask for a raise or take more money out of your business as the owner, you'll be in trouble. Your boss will just look for one of the many other people who can do your job and will do it for your current compensation. Or your business customers/patients will just go to one of the many other providers offering the same services for less. Either way, it's not good for you.

So, you need to focus on altering or evolving or adding to what you offer. Make it more unique. Create more value. Build new skills. Move to a new area. Ultimately, your goal is to make it so that you are doing something that very few other people are doing.

I'll use myself as a case example. When I was looking for my first job, I knew what average compensation was for a new plastic surgeon. This was an important part of knowing my value before entering contract negotiations as we discussed above. But I also knew that I was worth more money than this average salary. I knew that the value I brought was higher. At first, I knew this intrinsically. We all should believe in ourselves. However, I needed to prove this.

So, I went through my training, my skills, and my accomplishments. I separated out those that few other plastic surgeons possessed or accomplished. When I met with prospective jobs, I didn't even mention that things that I could do that every plastic surgeon can do. What's the point? I led with and emphasized what I could bring that very few or no one else could. This includes super microsurgery, robotic surgery, lymphedema surgery, and advanced research. And that's how I increased my potential compensation.

Put simply, if we want to increase our clinical income, we need to:

- Actively acquire new skills or accomplishments to add value in ways that few others can
- Highlight those unique skills that are rarely possessed
- Seek opportunities in need of these rare value-adding skills and accomplishments
- Negotiate aggressively using the techniques discussed above

Understanding How You Are Compensated

After we wrap our heads around the philosophical strategies to increase compensation, we then need to fully understand how we get paid for our clinical work.

In my anecdotal estimation, the RVU compensation model is the most common model for physicians across the U.S. at least. When I was looking for my first job, most contracts came with an RVU compensation model. After this, the most common model is a collections or "profit and loss" model. To be honest, I didn't really understand these models all that well until even recently.

While a collections model is straightforward, we will review both models here with a main focus on the RVU system.

Collections Model

In a collections compensation model, the physician earns the difference between the money they bring in via their practice minus the expenses incurred in the utilization of their practice. There are no conversion factors or equations. You simply earn what you make minus what you spend—exactly the same as your personal net worth formula! The important distinction here is that you don't earn what you bill the patient or their insurance carrier. You earn only what you collect from what you bill.

This model may be more common in private practices although it can exist in the hospital or clinic setting for employed physicians as well.

RVU Model

RVU is an abbreviation for Relative Value Unit. And a Relative Value Unit is a numerical measure of value provided via some service, treatment, procedure, or other healthcare related event. Groups have determined the baseline value of 1 RVU and then they decided how many RVUs valued each healthcare related good/service. Therefore, RVUs are a replacement of the numerical and monetary value of a healthcare service (think office visit, procedure, surgery, etc....).

But not all RVUs are equal. First, there are "facility" RVUs and "non-facility" RVUs. Just throw facility RVUs right out the window. They are not for you. They are for the hospital/center/surgery center that you perform said healthcare service at or in.

And you may think that all non-facility RVUs are all for physicians. However, you would be incorrect. Within the non-facility RVUs, work RVUs (wRVUs) represent the "work" done by a particular physician in providing this service, treatment, procedure, or other healthcare related event. There are other RVUs like "practice expense" (PE) RVUs and malpractice RVUs as well (Fig. 13.1). So, the non-facility wRVUs that traditionally apply to physician compensation are just a portion of the entire "RVU pie" that comes from a patient's treatment or procedure.

An RVU (I will now be using RVU synonymously with non-facility wRVU) now needs a conversion factor to be translated into money generated from the medical event. It needs something to convert your work into money. These conversion factors use units of $/RVU.

Therefore your RVU compensation is set by the following equation:

$$\text{RVU}^* \, \$ \, / \, \text{RVU} = \textbf{Your Compensation} \text{ for any given medical service}$$

For example, the average $/RVU for plastic surgeons is around $65/RVU. So, if a plastic surgeon performs a widgetplasty (not a real surgery) valued at 20 wRVUs, their compensation for that service will be:

$$20 \, \text{RVU}^* \, \$65 \, / \, \text{RVU} = \$1,300$$

And the rest of the RVU pie is similarly sliced and divvied up.

		National		Global (Locality)	
	Facility:	$706.84		$706.84	
	Non-Facility:	$861.89		$861.89	
RVUs - Non-Facility		National		Global (Locality)	
	Work RVU:	9.9		9.9	
	PE RVU:	14.27		14.27	
	Malpractice RVU:	1.9		1.9	
	Total RVU:	26.07		26.07	
	Conversion Factor:	33.0607			
RVUs - Facility		National		Global (Locality)	
	Work RVU:	9.9		9.9	
	PE RVU:	9.58		9.58	
	Malpractice RVU:	1.9		1.9	
	Total RVU:	21.38		21.38	
	Conversion Factor:	33.0607			

Fig. 13.1 *RVU breakdown for a skin graft surgery*

Evaluating the RVU and Collections Compensation Models

So, we can see that overall, the RVU compensation model is also fairly simple and straightforward. But is it better than collections? Well, let's compare it to the other most prominent compensation model, a pure profit and loss (P&L) compensation model.

Advantages of the RVU System

- Easy to understand and track
- All that you need to do is figure out the RVU values of the services you provide and your $/RVU conversion factor
- Good for when patients don't have great insurance (or any)
- The RVU model doesn't depend on money actually coming in from insurance (or anywhere else)
- You are created for the RVU just by providing the service

- Good for when your practice does not have favorable rates for certain procedures with insurance companies

- Again, you make the RVUs from performing the procedure
- And you are paid based on your $/RVU conversion factor
- Those are the only factors that matter for your compensation

- Clear division of labor among partners who work together (surgeon, co-surgeon)

- This happens a lot in surgery in particular
- Me and my partners often operate together with one being the primary surgeon and the other being the "co-surgeon"
- When this is done with an RVU model, each surgeon receives 62.5% of the allowable amount (rather than both getting 100%)
- This is easier to track than divvying up cash.

  But there are disadvantages…

Disadvantages of the RVU Model

- RVU values are set by CMS

- But these values may or may not be adopted by private insurance companies & your practice depending on negotiations
- This means you could be paid for less RVUs than your practice gets paid

- $/RVU conversion factor is also set by CMS

- But again, this may not correlate well with how much your practice is getting paid or pays you for your work
- For instance, one contract offer of mine would only pay me $35/RVU rather than the average $65/RVU for plastic surgeons

- Traditionally worse for cash-based services

- For example, let's take aesthetic surgery; employees in an RVU model performing aesthetic surgery as an employee will typically make much less than colleagues in private practice accepting put of pocket cash payments
- This extends to many other medical services

- As a doctor, you only are compensated for non-facility wRVUs

- But didn't you bring the patient to the practice/clinic/surgery center/hospital and contribute to the overall facility RVUs being paid to them?

  There is really only one way to address all of these disadvantages. Unfortunately, it is something that we as physicians receive little to no training in. And we have not always done it very well. But we can learn to do it better and be very successful at it. The answer is to negotiate!

- If you are employed, negotiate set RVU values and $/RVU conversions with your practice or employer
- If you own your practice, negotiate RVU values and conversions with private insurance companies
- Negotiate cash-based medical service RVU values with your employer
- Negotiate additional compensation based on facility and non-work RVUs

Now, let's quickly shift gears to discuss how you will typically see RVUs appear in your first (and subsequent) contracts. Generally, first contracts come with:

- A base salary for the first year followed by,
- A base salary with RVU bonus above a certain RVU level (Example: you keep 30% of RVUs collected above 40,000 at a conversion factor of $50/RVU) followed by,
- A pure RVU structure after the third year (Example: you make $60/RVU generated)

And as an important note, this is common in all practice environments! This includes hospital-based and academic jobs for sure. But also private practice jobs if you are an employee of the practice. And with all of this said, you need to make sure that you know how to negotiate your compensation if it is with an RVU model…

Before agreeing to an RVU model for compensation make sure you know and understand:

- The negotiated RVU values for your most common medical services
- The exact $/RVU conversion factor you will be using
- How many RVUs the least busy person in the practice does annually
- How many RVUs the busiest person in the practice does annually
- And how many RVUs the last hire did in their first 3 years

Any hesitancy or refusal on the part of your potential practice to share any of this information is a big red flag.

In the end, why does all this matter? It matters for at least a few big reasons. For one, the equation to build wealth and achieve financial freedom is simple. You just need to increase and invest the margin between what you make and what you spend. And clinical compensation is the major contributor to "what you make" for most physicians. For two, you really need to know your value as a doctor. And understanding RVUs helps you to do that. And lastly, feeling like you receive fair compensation plays a big role in your clinical fulfillment, satisfaction, and freedom from burnout. This was big for me. It makes sense to understand compensation models and give this proper consideration in your practice!

Now let's discuss opportunities to increase your income via non-clinical routes!

Create Non-clinical Income

All physicians consciously think about their clinical income. However, the majority of doctors ignore the potential of non-clinical income to help build their wealth. Colloquially called "physician side gigs," streams of non-clinical income are available for all physicians and can have a major impact on your wealth building.

There are a ton of awesome advantages to physician side gigs

- Create passive income (money you make while you sleep)
- Diversify your income so that a decrease in one income stream does not create financial stress
- Increase your income!
- Decrease the amount of savings that you need to retire
- Pay off your debts faster
- Invest more
- Utilize tax breaks to your advantages
- Exercise your entrepreneurial muscles
- Spend intentionally on goods or services that bring you joy

Importantly, side gigs are not endeavors to complicate your life or to further take time away from your family. Most doctors worry that a side gig will result in them spending more of their time. In fact, they do the exact opposite. The important thing when deciding to pursue a side gig is to establish your long-term goals for it. My side gigs will allow me to practice medicine on my own terms, because I want to, not because I have to. They will give me more time with my family and for my personal well-being as they turn into passive income.

With this in mind, let's review some of the ways that doctors can leverage their medical expertise to create non-clinical streams of income.

Medical Surveys

This is a favorite of many physicians. I know some who have made tens of thousands of dollars annually from medical surveys. To get started, just register with a medical survey company. They will then begin sending you paid surveys related to your specialty and expertise.

Virtual Healthcare Consulting

Once I got involved with medical surveys, I began to receive more and more opportunities for formal virtual healthcare consulting with various healthcare companies and third-party facilitators. In general, for these opportunities you can set your own rate. I set my rate at $500/hour. I came up with this number as it is the amount I felt comfortable losing an hour of my evening for. Some opportunities don't match this and I pass them up. But this will be personal for everyone. These consulting sessions generally take place over Zoom or over the phone.

Expert Witness

As an expert witness, you are consulting for an attorney or client who needs your expertise in the legal sense. This is an opportunity that usually starts off by you reaching out or cold responding to an opportunity. You can also just reach out to various law firms to let them know of your interest and expertise. Once you get started and if you do a good job, you are very likely to get asked to help more and more in the future.

Industry and Medical Device Consulting

This option may include activities directly with a medical device company or a pharmaceutical company or with a third-party company such as McKinsey. Activities may involve:

- Lecturing
- Running sponsored trials
- Helping with product development
- Consulting on the medical landscape for products

There does exist a bit of a grey area here as working in such a capacity creates a bias that can have clinical and research implications. This does not mean that you should not take such an opportunity. If you truly believe in a device or drug or company and want to help, go for it. Just make sure your job is aware and that all proper disclosures are made.

Now comes the question of how to get in the door with these companies if you do have interest in this. The answer is that you need to put yourself out there and ask. In select cases, companies may approach you, but this is not the norm. So, if you do truly believe in a device, drug, or healthcare company and see yourself as a good fit to help them, then reach out and ask them to help. It may seem awkward, but I can guarantee that there are tons of companies out there looking for your knowledge and willing to pay for it.

Consulting for Other Physicians

This can take a variety of forms:

- Coaching other physicians
- Taking part time opportunities within healthcare administration
- Consulting with other practices to optimize patient acquisition or the business side of running as practice
- Teaching physicians a new skill
- Helping doctors or the healthcare system with any unique expertise that you have and they want

There is no limit here. You can work to identify any area of need or want for other doctors and use your expertise to help them. I know doctors who help other practices run better as a consultant. There are others who consult with hospital systems to reduce waste. Once you identify a niche and identify your passion to help other doctors, don't stop. Keep looking for opportunities and letting others know what you can offer.

Medical Device Creation

You can also invent and patten a medical device to sell. To do so, focus on a pain point in your practice. What do you wish existed to make your work easier? Once you have an idea, work with a medical or pharmaceutical manufacturer to bring your idea to life. Make sire to also work with a patent lawyer to protect your intellectual property.

Medical Chart Review

This side gig involves medical chart review for various healthcare organizations. In general, you will find these opportunities by reaching out to various organizations. Then, once your foot is in the door, you can set your own rate and will find more opportunities coming to you directly!

Insurance Review

Given the present reality of insurance companies and their role in our healthcare system, it is necessary for insurance companies to have access to good, compassionate, and smart physicians to help with their reviews. And currently, there is a big need for this, and the compensation is very good. Same as with all of the other opportunities, your best bet is to reach out to companies directly.

Medical Writing

Medical writing can come in various forms. Many physicians have successfully written fictional books covering plots both medical and non-medical. Writing a medical review book in your area of expertise is also a great option. If you are interested, I would recommend speaking to someone in your specialty's professional society and/or board to get started. Then find a medical publisher. Make sure to research other review books in your field to make sure you provide unique and comprehensive value.

Freelance medical writing is also in very high demand. You may not realize it but a lot of media outlets are always looking for content related to healthcare. In fact, you are an expert in a field that is of high interest to the public and with a relative paucity of other experts. Just connect to these sources to start getting some freelance work. You can cold e-mail outlets or sign up for a service like Help A Reporter Out (HARO) for daily emails with leads specific to healthcare topics.

Medical Content Creation

Again, there is a huge audience of both physicians and non-physicians for medical-related content. Work to identify a passion in a related area of healthcare. Then you can deliver that message through an online blog, podcast, social media, newsletter, or any other form. These side gigs generate income largely via sponsorships and affiliate partnerships.

For a full list of non-clinical side gigs for physicians, visit https://prudentplastic-surgeon.com/physician-side-gigs/.

As doctors, we are uniquely positioned to leverage our medical expertise to create additional sources of income. However, it is another completely non-medical side gig that can accelerate wealth building for physicians (and anyone else) perhaps more than anything else—real estate investing.

Chapter 14
How Doctors Can Successfully Invest in Real Estate

When I first came across the concept of physicians investing in real estate, my reaction was similar to most. I dismissed the idea. It seemed too complicated. I didn't know anything about real estate investing. It also seemed like it required a lot of money and time; two things that I did not have readily available as a fresh attending physician.

However, as I discovered more and more physicians successfully investing in real estate to build their wealth and reach financial freedom, my mindset began to shift. Instead of thinking, "I can't do this," I began thinking, "If other doctors can do this, why can't I?"

Thanks to this mindset shift and a self-education in real estate investing, my wife and I now own 7 investment properties totalling 15 doors after 2 years. These investments bring in a cash flow of ~$10,000 each month and have grown our net worth by 7 figs. I include these numbers not to boast, there are many physicians making much greater gains. I share these numbers instead to show what is possible via real estate investing even for a full-time physician who started out knowing nothing about it, like me. I hope that this example demonstrates two things: real estate investing is a true wealth accelerant and if I can do it, you can as well!

This chapter is not an exhaustive review of real estate investing. Instead, my goal is to introduce the basic concepts and strategies of real estate investing to demonstrate how it grows your wealth and how you can get started.

To begin, regardless of exact investing strategy, there are 5 major ways that real estate investing grows your wealth:

- Cash flow
- Appreciation
- Tax benefits
- Equity Build Up (by paying down the mortgage)
- Hedging inflation (rents increase as inflation increases)

© The Author(s), under exclusive license to Springer Nature
Switzerland AG 2023
J. D. Frey, *Money Matters in Medicine*,
https://doi.org/10.1007/978-3-031-27300-1_14

For now, let's just focus on the first two, cash flow and appreciation. While the others are certainly beneficial, cash flow and appreciation are where most wealth potential is concentrated. As a definition, real estate cash flow is the income that an investment property generates above its expenses. This cash flow is generally in the form of rent in excess of expenses like mortgage payments, maintenance, and the like. Meanwhile, appreciation is s growth in perceived value of an investment from when you buy the property to when you sell it. An example would be buying a property for $100,000 and selling it for $200,000 3 years later.

In general terms, you should be investing in real estate for cash flow, not appreciation. Expected appreciation can be the cherry on top of an investment property with great cash flow. But you should not invest for appreciation alone. The reason is that any property's value on the real estate market can fluctuate greatly and arbitrarily, much like an individual stock. Investing for appreciation is therefore really speculating, not investing.

On the flip side, when you invest in a property for its cash flow potential, the whims of the real estate market do not matter to you. If your property cash flows $1500 each month after expenses, it will continue to do so whether the market values the property at $100,000 or $200,000. A strong real estate investing strategy will therefore focus on creating and maintaining cash flow. In fact, for larger investment properties, higher income can even help increase what is called *forced appreciation* which is not at the whim of the market.

Now that we understand how real estate can generate wealth, let's review some of the basic different ways that someone can invest in real estate.

In broad terms, this real estate investing guide will be broken down into:

- Active real estate investing and
- Passive real estate investing

Passive Real Estate Investing

Passive real estate investing is any investment into real estate that you make with your money alone. You contribute no "sweat equity" to the investment. You contribute your investment (money) to someone else (usually a group of other investors). They then use the accumulated monies to buy and run investment property(ies). The most common forms of this type of real estate investing are *syndications* and *funds*.

In a syndication, you and several other investors pool your money to buy and invest in one property. In a fund, you are contributing along with others to a large pool of money used to invest in many real estate investment properties. If you performed your due diligence well with the passive investment that you choose, they do well, and you receive a return based on the structure of your investment. These investments can use Buy & Hold, Buy & Sell, Fix & Flip, or any other real estate strategy to turn a profit. They are all passive in this instance because you are not the one doing the work. The sponsors of the syndication or fund are doing the work.

As you can see, there are advantages to passive real estate investing. For one, you don't have to contribute any sweat equity to the investment. You contribute your money and when the investment does well, you get paid.

The flip side to this, however, is that the performance of the investment is decidedly **not** in your control. You had better be sure that you trust the syndication or fund that you are giving the money to. Because if the investment loses, you don't get any profits and lose your money as well. For this reason, it is extremely important to perform extensive due diligence on these investments before going into one. That's why I would argue that these investments are not truly passive, but rather are leveraged. The problem here is that any past performance cannot guarantee future performance and again, there is little control. These funds will often set out *pro forma* or expected returns. But these are *estimates*. They have no responsibility to live up to these returns.

Lastly, the real money in these investments is going to the people who *are* putting in the sweat equity. Of course, the active partners of the fund or syndication are going to set things up so that they see most profits if the investment performs well. This is only fair. You're paying a big tax in exchange for being able to be passive in the investment. And, while we're on the topic of taxes, depending on the type of passive investment, some of the tax benefits of real estate investing don't pass to you as a passive investor.

Active Real Estate Investing

Active real estate investing, in the meantime, is any form of real estate investing in which you are actively involved. This doesn't necessarily mean that you swing the sledgehammer or fix the toilet. But you are involved in the operations of your real estate business. There are many forms of active real estate investing. These include:

- Buy & Hold,
- Buy & Sell,
- Buy, Fix, & Sell,
- Buy, Rent, & Hold, etc.

The commonality here is that all these pursuits require your active attention beyond just writing a check.

Active investing allows the investor to adjust and personalize the amount of control that she wants over her investments. She can buy a property, rent it out, and self-manage the property. Or she can buy that same property, hire a property management company, and just get a profit/loss statement every month. This can be adjusted anywhere along the spectrum and changed at any time. You can even just automate operations, so you manage the property with minimal effort. This is what I do. Most importantly, in active investing, the profits all go to you. You can then decide if you want to pay employees to defray some of the hassle or if you want to just pay yourself.

With that primer set, I'll share my preferred strategy for active real estate investing. My wife and I have chosen to focus on Buy, Rent, & Hold multifamily investment properties.

There are several reasons that we decided on each of these sub-strategies:

1. **Buy**—Well, you can't own real estate without buying it so there's step #1
2. **Rent**—By renting the properties, we can have the tenants pay our mortgage with their rents. In addition, since the total rents exceed the mortgage/tax/insurance/ etc. payments, we keep the extra money as *cash flow*.
3. **Hold**—The overall real estate market is not unlike the stock market. They both go up and down in the short term. However, in the long term, they generally go up. So, in buying properties that cash flow and holding them for a long time, we can increase the chance that the property gains value by the time we eventually plan to sell it.
4. **Multifamily**—By increasing the number of units under one roof, you decrease the cost per unit, increase profit in general, and make your business more efficient. Right now, we are starting with 2-4 unit properties but will go bigger in the future.

Meanwhile, cash-on-cash return is our metric of choice. There are a ton of different metrics to evaluate real estate properties and they all depend on what you are hoping to get out of them. For us, cash flow is number one.

The way to measure cash flow is a cash-on-cash return calculation where:

$$Cash - on - cash = Yearly\ cash\ flow$$
$$/\ Amount\ of\ money\ that\ you\ put\ into\ the\ property$$

In this equation,

- Note that the yearly cash flow is the amount of cash you make each year after all expenses including mortgage, insurance, etc. are paid, and
- The amount of money that you put into the property is the exact amount that actually came out of your pocket

For instance, if I bought a $100,000 property with a mortgage and 20% down with $5000 of closing costs, the denominator in the above equation (amount of money out of my pocket) would be $25,000. If the property cash flowed $2500/year, $2500 is my numerator. And my cash-on-cash return would be 10%.

Our goal is to find properties that will cash flow >10%. Most properties will not meet this goal off the bat. Instead, we look for ways to tap hidden value—ways to increase rent or decrease expenses—that others don't see in order to reach our goal of >10%.

At this point, some of you may wonder, "That cash flow doesn't seem like that much...is it worth it?" Don't be fooled by the initial numbers. One property will not make you wealthy. In fact, the cash flow from one investment property is usually a drop in the bucket compared to a physician's income. But we are not in it for one property.

Let's go back to our example property. We buy it at $100,000 for 20% down with a 15-year mortgage and have $5000 in closing costs. After monthly expenses, we cash flow about $208/month for an annual cash flow of $2500. We save this extra cash flow each month to reinvest in future real estate. In 15 years, the property is ours, free and clear, as the last mortgage payment is made.

In those 15 years, we would have continued making cash flow each month. Plus, the mortgage is now paid off completely by our tenants. That means we have 100% equity in the property. Plus, the property likely appreciated in market value over that long time period (15 years) due to the upward trend of the overall real estate market. Now we can take the money we made from cash flow to buy another bigger property and repeat the process.

But there's more, let's say that instead of buying one property in the beginning, we saved and bought one each year. Now, say we used advanced techniques like *forced appreciation* to increase our cash flow and market value so we could sell the property at a profit sooner than 15 years. Let's say when we sell our properties, we do so using a 1031 exchange for another property so that any capital gains are tax-free.

Then, let's say with each property, we take advantage of *cost segregation/bonus depreciation* to claim paper losses despite accumulating real profits from our real estate business. Now we have passive losses to offset passive gains on your taxes. Or even better, let's say we claim Real Estate Professional tax status and can claim these paper losses against our W2 income. This would save us tens or hundreds of thousands of dollars in taxes. *But this is how wealth is created!*

The important thing to remember when considering active and passive real estate investing is that there is no right answer. There is only the right answer *for you.*

In starting this chapter, I said that real estate investing is a great investment vehicle for all doctors. And it is. It's not to say there are no downsides. There are downsides—due diligence, work, time—but they are worth it. I have seen how real estate investing has changed my financial well-being and wealth for the better.

So perhaps the question is not *if* real estate investing works for you, but rather, *how* can it work for you? Take some time to think over the factors I've included here and think about which strategy is best for you. If you prefer a completely hands off approach, learn how to perform due diligence on deal sponsors and consider passive real estate investments. If investing actively is your preference, learn how to analyze potential deals and meet with various investor real estate agents. The key is to get started!

Now, let's shift gears to discuss an important topic to help us preserve our wealth as we build it...

Chapter 15
A Primer on Taxes

Nobody really likes taxes. Some people hate them. Some people accept them. But no one likes them. However, that is not a reason to ignore taxes. Understanding how taxes work puts you in control. Remember, you need to pay the amount you legally owe in taxes, but you don't need to leave the government a tip. With this in mind, let's review how our progressive tax system works and how that knowledge can help us come tax time.

Keep in mind, until the past couple of years, I ignored my taxes. The result was that I often did leave a tip for the government. In fact, paying attention to my taxes and understanding how the progressive tax system works has resulted in huge savings and will accelerate my path to financial freedom.

And one last thing before I start, this chapter has nothing to do with if I think the current tax system is right or wrong. Honestly, I have no idea. Do I love paying high taxes now? No. But there was a time during my training when I did use government assistance when we struggled. I also use public programs today. My argument is this: Taxes are a reality of our life. Whether we agree with them or not, we still need to understand them. To ignore them out of spite only hurts us.

To begin, we live in a country with a progressive tax system. A progressive tax system taxes citizens based on their ability to pay said taxes. Basically, it means that people with lower incomes pay less taxes and people with higher incomes pay higher taxes. This contrasts with a flat tax system where everyone pays the same percentage of income in taxes. For completeness' sake, a regressive tax system is one in which the same rate applies to all regardless of ability to pay. This is what a sales tax is.

So, what exactly do we need to understand about our progressive tax system as high-income earning physicians?

First, all our income isn't taxed at the same rate. This is the hallmark of a progressive tax system. Yet the misconception that all of our money is taxed at the same rate persists. Again, I didn't understand this concept until I started learning about taxes as part of my financial education.

© The Author(s), under exclusive license to Springer Nature Switzerland AG 2023
J. D. Frey, *Money Matters in Medicine*,
https://doi.org/10.1007/978-3-031-27300-1_15

The way that we are taxed is via tax brackets. Meaning that the first $1 of our income is not taxed at the same rate as out last $1. As the chart below shows, in 2022 our first $10,275 of income (if filing single) was taxed at 10%. Meanwhile, if we filed single and make $539,900 of more, our last $1 was being taxed at 37% (Fig. 15.1).

Once we understand this, we can recognize that stepping down in tax brackets will save us enormously come tax time. And there are ways to do this. The name of this game is reducing our taxable income. And we can accomplish this through various tax deductions. As opposed to tax credits that decrease our taxes in a $1: $1 fashion (and are better than tax deductions), tax deductions allow us to decrease the amount of our income that gets taxed.

By maximizing deductions available to ourselves like maximizing our 401 k retirement accounts, we decrease our taxable income within our marginal (top) tax bracket. This is a great help. But even better, if we drop down a tax bracket, the savings become even greater. And fair or not, remember that employees (like myself) have less tax deductions available to use than business owners like private practice physicians. You can get around this by running your own side business so that you can use these deductions to your advantage.

Next, we must grasp that our average and marginal tax rates are different. In a progressive tax system, there is a difference between our average tax rate and our marginal tax rate. Our average tax rate is simply the averaged rate that we paid for

2022 Federal Income Tax Brackets and Rates for Single Filers, Married Couples Filing Jointly, and Heads of Households

Tax Rate	For Single Filers	For Married Individuals Filing Joint Returns	For Heads of Households
10%	$0 to $10,275	$0 to $20,550	$0 to $14,650
12%	$10,275 to $41,775	$20,550 to $83,550	$14,650 to $55,900
22%	$41,775 to $89,075	$83,550 to $178,150	$55,900 to $89,050
24%	$89,075 to $170,050	$178,150 to $340,100	$89,050 to $170,050
32%	$170,050 to $215,950	$340,100 to $431,900	$170,050 to $215,950
35%	$215,950 to $539,900	$431,900 to $647,850	$215,950 to $539,900
37%	$539,900 or more	$647,850 or more	$539,900 or more

Source: Internal Revenue Service

Fig. 15.1 2022 Income Tax Brackets in the United States

our entire income based on this tiered progressive system. Meanwhile, our marginal tax rate however is the tax rate on our last $1 of earned income.

I think this is important to understand on an emotional level. Too many people tell me that the government takes 40% of their paycheck for federal taxes. First, this just isn't true given the current tax brackets that don't go that high. But even if they did, all of your income isn't taxed at that top rate...only your income above the designated level ($539,900 for this filing as single). Again, your marginal tax rate isn't your average tax rate.

The other emotional argument I hear is that we just shouldn't work once we reach a certain income because the taxes are too high. While I understand the frustration, this just doesn't add up. Do I want to keep 100% of my money? Yes. But I'll take 60% of it over 0% any day of the week.

But there's a more practical reason this is helpful to understand. Since our average and marginal tax rates differ, we can take advantage of tax rate arbitrage in an effort to lower our taxes. By deferring extra income during already high-income years to potentially lower income future years, we can minimize the amount of income we have in our marginal tax bracket. This will also serve to lower our average tax rate. This is one of the huge advantages with tax deferred retirement accounts like 401 k's. We defer our income during peak income years into a 401 k. This amount is therefore deducted from our income for tax purposes. Then, we withdraw that money later in life (when we theoretically are earning less or not at all in retirement). Thus, we have shifted income from a higher tax bracket to a lower tax bracket and saved money on taxes.

The last important concept to understand about our progressive tax system is that it permits reduced tax burden on those who can least afford it. This has been implied above. But those with lower income pay lower taxes because they are in lower tax brackets.

And due to the basic principle above, progressive tax systems keep more money in the pocket of those with lower incomes. This ensures that they have enough money to live their lives and to spend on goods and services. This is good for the overall economy. It is also good for physicians. We don't have a universal healthcare system. This means that on top of insurance, patients must pay out of pocket in variable amounts for healthcare. As doctors we unfortunately know that socioeconomic factors limit access to healthcare as well as patients' willingness to seek healthcare. More money in people's pockets who needs it helps keep them healthier and keeps them coming to see us as physicians. Oversimplified? Maybe. A win-win? I think so.

In the end, taxes are here. And they aren't going anywhere anytime soon. They will always go up and down slightly depending on politics, but they will never go away. That means that it is up to us to understand how they work and what we can do to make sure we only pay what we owe. Understanding our progressive tax system and what that means for us is a really important first step.

The next step is employing strategies to reduce your taxes. As I mentioned above, when you are an employee, your opportunities to lower your tax burden are much less than a business owner. You are not able to deduct business expenses. In fact, after the 2017 Tax Cuts & Jobs Act, you are no longer able to deduct non-reimbursed business expenses as an employed physician. You also can't deduct home offices, car mileage, or take advantage of the 20% QBI tax deduction.

So, the main strategy as a W2 physicians when it comes to taxes is to reduce your taxable income as much as possible. Your gross income is what you make pre-tax. But not all of that is taxed. Your taxable income is your income after all tax credits and deductions have been accounted for. So, the name of the game is to lower that taxable income as much as possible. There are three main strategies we will discuss. However, along with these 3 strategies, you will obviously want to make sure you maximize more obvious tax credits and deductions like the child tax credit etc. However, high income earners realize very minimal benefits from these.

The first was mentioned above, maximizing tax advantaged retirement accounts.

When you contribute to a tax deferred retirement account, the money that you put in is not taxed. And that contribution amount is subtracted from your gross income to lower your taxable income. Plus, the money grows tax free. But it is taxed upon withdrawal of course. However, the tax advantages up front are important.

Examples of these types of retirement accounts include:

- 401k/403b
- 457
- HSA
- 529 (Sometimes)

I say that a 529 is sometimes a tax advantaged retirement account because money goes in post-tax, comes out non-taxed, and grows tax free if it is used on education costs for a beneficiary. But in many states, there is a tax deduction for contributions. So, it can make sense to lower your taxable income this way if you have children and live in such a state. But remember, if you don't use the withdrawals for education related expenses, then you get hit with a 10% penalty on withdrawal. So that makes it not worth it in that case.

The next strategy is tax loss harvesting. This is a powerful concept. When your investments in the stock market drop, you can sell them (for a loss) and then buy another investment that is not substantially identical. Why would anyone do this?

Well, by selling your investment that has lost money, you lock in a loss. But you then buy a similar, but not substantially identical, investment so that you maintain your asset allocation. This way, your loss is only a paper loss. You still own essentially the same investments in the same amount.

Each year, you can deduct $3000 of these paper losses from tax loss harvesting from your taxable income. If you have more paper losses, these can offset passive gains now or in the future. But it will not reduce your W2 income any more than this $3000.

But still, this is a good way to further lower your taxes for W2 physicians.

Lastly, a more advanced way to significant lower your taxes, whether W2 or not is via real estate with Real Estate Professional Status. An important part of what makes REI so great are the tax advantages available to investors. That is because real estate undergoes depreciation which creates large passive losses on properties that in real life are making cash flow.

You can use these passive losses from real estate to offset passive gains. But this does not really help W2 physicians to lower their taxes. Because it does not offset active income…unless you or your spouse have attained Real Estate Professional Status or REPS. With REPS, these passive losses can now reduce your taxable active income by a ton! However, attaining REPS is not simple. But it took a lot of work and requires at least 750 hours of material participation in your real estate business.

Beyond these tax saving strategies for employed physicians, even more opportunities to reduce their tax burden exist for self-employed doctors or doctors with side businesses. The beauty is that you don't have to start your own medical practice to do this. You may be like me and be very happy in your employed W2 doctor job. In that case, start a small business for a side gig. Even something as small as a business for completing medical surveys.

When you do this, a whole new world up for you tax wise!

Now you can deduct:

- A home office
- Car mileage
- Renting your home out to your business
- Business expenses
- Business trips
- Meals
- Per diems
- And more

Additionally, you can use different tax-advantaged retirement accounts available to self-employed individuals like a solo 401 k, cash balance plan, or others to defer taxes.

Understanding taxes and creating a strategy to minimize your tax burden as a high-income earner is crucial. Some of these concepts are simple and can be done without professional assistance by the interested physician. Others however are more complex and are better outsourced. And this is by no means an exhaustive list. Other great tax advantaged opportunities may be fitting in your situation! Regardless, consider your personal circumstances and consider consulting with a tax advisor familiar with high income earners.

We have come a long way and covered a lot of exciting ground in the past 15 chapters. Now it is time to tie everything together into our own personalized written financial plan. This can seem daunting at first. But don't worry. We will walk through the process in the next chapter using my own financial plan as a guide so that you can create your own!

Chapter 16
Putting your Personal Plan Together

Selenid and I drafted our first written financial plan a few months after we started our financial education. Once we educated ourselves enough, we realized that our written financial plan was the next logical step to tie everything together. It took us a few months to do this as we sought information from various resources and sifted through to find good advice. Hopefully this book will accelerate this process for you!

Regardless, after creating our written financial plan, something unexpected happened. With a financial plan in place, my financial well-being shot through the roof. I was still in training, making the same salary (not much). My wife was still finishing her PhD without an income. We lived in NYC with two young children and high expenses. My debt remained at approximately $500,000. I worked the same long hours. However, I now had a plan that I knew would lead me to reach financial freedom on my terms. My burnout improved significantly, and I was able to focus more on what I loved about medicine. I became a better doctor!

This experience was nothing short of an epiphany leading to multiple revelations. Many of these I have shared through this book—such as the myth of money as a malignant topic for physicians. One of the more profound revelations from this epiphany was just how important a written financial plan can be. It is a simple written document with an incredibly outweighed impact.

Selenid and I still refer to our written plan to this day. It continues to guide us on our journey to financial freedom. This is why I encourage all doctors, regardless of career stage, to craft their own written financial plan. The task can seem daunting. But like everything else in this book, it is actually fairly simple when you break it down. And that is exactly what we are going to do.

Together, let's go through Selenid and my actual original written personal financial plan, section by section. Nothing has been edited or omitted. The only things that have changed are that some goals have been reached since we originally wrote this. After each section, we will review what is included in the section and why as well as how you can personalize it to your own unique financial and life circumstances.

© The Author(s), under exclusive license to Springer Nature
Switzerland AG 2023
J. D. Frey, *Money Matters in Medicine*,
https://doi.org/10.1007/978-3-031-27300-1_16

Our financial plan is not "right." But it is right for us. The goal here is not for you to just use our financial plan and fit it into your life. Instead, use this financial plan as a template or jumping off point. Keep what you like. Throw away what you don't. My hope is for it to serve as a foundation for you to build your own path to financial freedom. So let's begin!

Selenid and Jordan's Financial Plan

Financial Priority List

1. Pay down high interest loans/debt (>8%)
2. Establish emergency fund (3–6 month's expenses)
3. Maximize employer 403(b) retirement account
4. Pay down medium interest loans (6–8%)
5. Invest in vetted real estate (cash flowing rentals w/ cash-on-cash ratio > 10%)
6. Contribute to 529 college savings account
7. Maximize 457(b) retirement account
8. Pay extra to mortgage
9. Pay down low interest loans (<3%)
10. Contribute to back door/spousal Roth IRA (every January if contributing—2 steps)
11. Contribute to retirement taxable account
12. Donate to charity with equity dividends

This first section is a priority list of where we want our saved money to go. Each item is like a bucket. We fill the bucket until it is full. Then the money spills into the next bucket. And on and on down the list. Currently, we reach until item #6. Then our money runs out. As we will those buckets more, more money will spill into the more downstream items.

You can see that are very interested in aggressively paying off our loans and our priorities reflect that here. You will also notice that investing in cash flowing real estate is very high on our list at #5. This means it is basically the third bucket that our money goes into after maximizing my main employer retirement accounts and paying down debt.

General Financial Guidelines

- Save at least 30% of income every year (includes debt payments)
- Review and square budget on the first of every month
- We will calculate our net worth every 2–4 months
- We will calculate our savings rate and our total return and real return each year

- We'll use our credit card only once balance is at $0. At that point, we will use it for everyday purchases and will pay it off in full every month
- We will not use credit to purchase automobiles, appliances, or vacations
- We will use credit only for mortgages

This next section lists the general "rules" of our financial plan. These are things that we agree that we "have to" do. There is no argument when it comes to these items. We do them without thinking. Our goal savings rate is still at least 30% although it currently is greater than 43%. Note that we also check our net worth every 2–4 months to assess where we are and make sure we are following the rules of the wealth building game.

Specific Financial Goals

- Pay off consumer debt in 2 years (2022)
- Pay off student debt in 5 years (2025)
- We will be worth $one million in 12 years (2033)
- Save $40,000 to buy car 1 in 3 years (2023), save $40,000 to buy car 2 in 6 years (2026)
- Save enough to cash flow at least $250,000 in retirement (goal retirement at least 2045)

    - This will be via hybrid approach using equity and real estate investing
    - Save $1–two million in equities for 4% yearly withdrawal of ~$71,000
    - Cash flow >$200,000 from real estate investments in 5 years (2025)

- Save $400,000 for kids' college tuition
- Save $250,000 for renovation/down payment new home
- The mortgage on the home we are living in will be paid off when we retire

This section delineates our specific financial goals. I am a believer in goal-setting. Goals should be specific and should be big. To the end, you will note that we listed time points for our goals. This is important. Then, once you have a goal, all that is left to do is plot the course. Without a goal, you'll never arrive at one. Main goals include debt pay off and our cash flow plan for retirement has not changed.

A lot of people ask me how we came up with this number. As we discussed in Chap. 8, we estimated our expenses in retirement knowing that we will not have to save for retirement, not need life or disability insurance, not be paying for our kids' education along with other expenses. But really, how can we forecast that far into the future? We can't accurately. So, we estimated a way bigger number than we will likely need. Again, I'd much rather overestimate than underestimate. You rnumbers should reflect your circumstances, your estimates, and your risk tolerance. I would like to believe that we will reach these goals ahead of schedule if we stay on course. However, we are keeping them the same for now.

General Investment Plans

- Our primary equity investment vehicles will be stock index mutual funds and bond index mutual funds, preferably within tax-sheltered accounts

  - These will primarily be funded through Jordan's income
  - We will strive to minimize the effects of taxes and expenses on our investment returns
  - In general, we will favor passively managed investments over actively managed investments

- Our primary real estate investment vehicle will be cash flowing rental investment properties with goal 10% cash-on-cash return to reach our real estate goals

  - This will primarily be funded by Selenid's income, Jordan's bonus, and monthly surplus
  - All cash flow from real estate will be re-invested in real estate

- We will strive to achieve a real return of at least 6% per year, averaged over our investment lifetime
- In a market downturn or bear market, we will not panic and sell low; however, we will try to use any truly extra cash (not emergency fund, etc.) to rebalance by buying more stock (or other depressed equity)
- We will tax loss harvest any losses >$3000 each year
- We will create a will in 2022
- Once we are 50 years old or our net worth is >$one million, we will meet with an estate planning attorney

Here are some general guidelines for our investment strategies. We use a hybrid approach with both equity and real estate investing. For equity investing, we use only broadly diversified low-cost index funds. For real estate investing, cash flowing rental properties with >10% cash-on-cash returns remain our primary vehicle.

Note our instructions for what to do when a bear market hits, which is… do nothing. This concept seems simple enough before you have a lot of skin in the game. However, it can be much more difficult to follow when you're losing your actual money. But remember, we're long-term investors, not speculators. Long-term, the overall stock market is a safe investment. No need to fret over the short term. Writing this out in your financial plan and referring to it in tough markets can save you millions of dollars and years of retirement.

Equity Asset Allocations

- Maintain an 80/20 stock/bond allocation, decreasing progressively to at least 60/40 by retirement
- Our primary asset classes will be domestic stock mutual funds, international stock mutual funds, and US Government bond mutual funds

- Our equity allocation will include domestic, international, and emerging market stocks and large-cap, mid-cap, and small/micro-cap stocks.

  – We will also allocate a percentage to REITs and other alternative asset classes if they promise diversification benefits and solid long-term returns
  – For the most part, these will be broad total market index funds, but they may be supplemented by small amounts of value index funds as needed to maintain a slight value tilt.

- Our bond allocation will be split 50/50 between nominal bonds and inflation-indexed bonds in tax-sheltered accounts as much as possible.
- Our pre-2020 Roth IRAs and 457 will remain target retirement funds and NOT count towards overall asset allocation
- Our emergency fund will be in high-yield savings accounts
- We will rebalance once each year (July) by buying more stocks/bonds as dictated to maintain goal allocation

Initial Asset Allocation

- 40% US Stocks
- 35% International Stocks
- 5% REITs
- 10% US Bonds
- 10% Inflation indexed bonds

You can review my actual investing portfolio at https://prudentplasticsurgeon.com/403b-investment-account/

Here, we list out exactly how we are going to invest our money in equities. Based on the rule of thumb we discussed in Chap. 8, my bond allocation based on age would be 30%. However, I have a slightly higher risk tolerance than this, so we moved our bond percentage to 20% and split it evenly between US bonds and inflation indexed bonds. In terms of stocks, we created a near even split between US and international stock index funds. We also believe in real estate as an asset class and thus included 5% of REIT funds.

There are innumerable excellent asset allocations. As I discussed in Chap. 8, even a simple three fund allocation of US and international stock index funds and a bond index fund is fantastic. The key is to invest broadly and passively in low cost, broadly diversified index funds based on your individual risk tolerance. Then rebalance yearly back to your goal asset allocation. Remember, investing is an individual game. You are not competing against anyone else. Your goals alone are what matter!

Future Changes

- Any change to our financial goals must be agreed upon by both Jordan and Selenid after careful consideration of short- and long-term benefits and risks
- Any change to these investment percentages or change in funds used will require a 3-month waiting period
- Development of any new asset class or new funds allowing us to invest in an asset class such as international small or international value stocks will require a 3-month waiting period prior to transferring funds

This is the last and likely most important section of our written personal financial plan. It is also evergreen. This section delineates how changes will and, more importantly, won't be made to this plan. This section is also where you may like to write out what you will *not* do when investing. This can come in handy if you are prone to get excited about new investing fads or hot trends. A written plan is only as good as your execution of it. There is no purpose to a plan that is constantly changing. Your plan is your foundation in the journey to financial freedom. It is the treasure map. So, you need to protect it.

When you design your financial plan, you want to do so calmly and without emotion. Then, we emotion strikes in the future due to a prolonged bear market or a hot new investment tip, you can refer to this document and remember why you are doing what you are doing. You can look at your goals and be reassured that you are on track to reach them with no need to jump on a new fad investment or succumb to short term pressures. That is why Selenid and I call for at least a three-month waiting period before any changes to our financial plan. If a new investment is good, it will still be good in 3 months. If we don't still think it's good in 3 months, then it likely never was. So far, we have not needed to change our written plan since we created it. We may change it in the future. But if so, it will only be after following these rules.

After this review, take some time to consider and review the different sections of a written financial plan. Think informally about your financial goals and priorities. If you have a partner, I strongly encourage you both to do this together. Then, when you have some time, sit together, and begin to write out your actual plan. You can start from scratch or use this one as a template. The goal is not to get it perfect the first time around. You may even take a few sessions to complete it like Selenid and I did. In fact, it may never be perfect. The beauty is that it does not need to be perfect to work. It just needs to be. Because it is simply a tangible reflection of your values and goals for you to refer to and use as a guiding force.

I may even dare to say that the process of creating your financial plan can be fun. I know that we really enjoyed thinking about and planning our financial freedom.

With your written financial plan in tow, you are now ready to set off on your path to financial well-being and freedom. The best part is that you can do so while keeping your focus where it belongs—on your family, friends, passions, and patients!

Epilogue: What's Next for You as a Financially Free Doctor?

Congratulations! You now have all the tools that you need to achieve financial freedom and become a financially free physician. The question then becomes not *if* you will ever reach financial freedom, but rather what will you do *when* you reach financial freedom?

Such a simple question can seem very heavy. But in fact, you already know the answer. Because you know your "*why*" for all of this. That is why, before we talked about any of the simple financial strategies, we determined our *why* way back in Chap. 4. Without that *why*, the question of what we will do as financially free physicians can seem like a monolith; like another call to arbitrarily define ourselves and our lives. In reality, this question was the very thing guiding us from the beginning.

Remember, my *why* for achieving financial freedom is *to gain financial well-being to enhance my overall well-being, to spend more time with family and friends, and to pursue my passions (including medicine) on my terms.*

If your why is cloudy or you feel it needs a refresher, re-read Chap. 4. Reflect either alone or with an accountability partner on your values, goals, and priorities in all aspects of life. The answer to this question will come into focus.

And so, what will you do as a financially free physician?

It is an exciting and freeing concept to consider. It's also completely personal. Like so many of the concepts that we have discussed, there are no right or wrong choices, just what is right for you. And that will depend on your – you guessed it – values, goals, and priorities.

For some financially free doctors, the answer will be to hang up the white coat. And that is perfectly fine. For others, the answer will be to continue in medicine either at the same or a reduced capacity. I plan to continue in medicine when I reach financial freedom. And that does not negate or undermine the point of working to achieve financial freedom. I know myself. And I know that I am much happier doing something because I *want* to and not because I *have* to – even if I love the thing that I am doing. Financial freedom also gives me the flexibility to adapt to changes in my professional environment without worrying about "sticking out a bad situation" simply for the money.

Beyond these considerations, I also believe there is a higher calling for financially free physicians – whether inside or outside of medicine. And that is to educate present and future physicians on the importance of and strategies to achieve financial well-being. Without fully dispelling the myth of money as "bad" in medicine, there will always be physicians suffering from a lack of financial well-being and the burnout it contributes to – like myself.

However, this goes even further beyond the important and sufficient goal of physician financial and overall well-being. I truly believe that a country and world of financially free doctors would change healthcare for the better in ways that we cannot even currently conceive. Let's consider this for a moment.

Financially free doctors are better doctors. This naturally leads to better patient care. Further, financially free doctors can untether from the maladaptive systems – insurance systems, administrative systems, and the like - currently limiting the ideal practice of medicine. Financially free doctors can protest and resist without fear of loss of income. A nation or world of financially free doctors can re-balance the scales, placing power back within the hands of the care givers. A world of financially free physicians can recreate these systems, and in turn the healthcare system, for the better of patients and doctors alike.

As I write, such a world seems far away. But this need not be the case. You now know how to create and travel your own path to financial freedom as a physician. You know it is not scary, intimidating, or even that complex using the simple strategies in this book. You can be confident that you *will* be a financially free (and better for it) physician. That means you can now teach other doctors how to do the same thing. And then they can pass it on. And so forth. Suddenly, such a world seems not only plausible but inevitable.

By picking up and reading this book, you have already completed the most difficult step - starting. I encourage you to keeping taking the next small step…and the next…and the one after that. Stack and celebrate small victories on your journey. Soon the steps will get easier, and you will be running on the path you have laid out for yourself. Financial well-being and freedom are worth it. You are worth it. Your patients are worth it. And medicine is worth it.

Thank you for sharing your path and journey with me.

Index